A Hundred Himalayas

WRITERS ON WRITING
Jay Parini, Series Editor

A good writer is first a good reader. Looking at craft from the inside, with an intimate knowledge of its range and possibilities, writers also make some of our most insightful critics. With this series we will bring together the work of some of our finest writers on the subject they know best, discussing their own work and that of others, as well as concentrating on craft and other aspects of the writer's world.

Poet, novelist, biographer, and critic, Jay Parini is the author of numerous books, including *The Apprentice Lover* and *One Matchless Time: A Life of William Faulkner*. Currently he is D. E. Axinn Professor of English & Creative Writing at Middlebury College.

TITLES IN THE SERIES

Michael Collier
Make Us Wave Back: Essays on Poetry and Influence

Nancy Willard
The Left-Handed Story: Writing and the Writer's Life

Christopher Benfey
American Audacity: Literary Essays North and South

Ilan Stavans
A Critic's Journey

Richard Stern
Still on Call

C. P. Cavafy
Selected Prose Works

Sydney Lea
A Hundred Himalayas: Essays on Life and Literature

A Hundred Himalayas

Essays on Life and Literature

Sydney Lea

The University of Michigan Press

Ann Arbor

Copyright © 2012 by Sydney Lea
All rights reserved
Published in the United States of America by
The University of Michigan Press
Manufactured in the United States of America
♾ Printed on acid-free paper

2015   2014   2015   2012   4   3   2   1

A CIP catalog record for this book is available from the British Library.

Library of Congress Cataloging-in-Publication Data

Lea, Sydney, 1942–
    A hundred Himalayas : essays on life and literature / Sydney Lea.
        p.   cm. — (Writers on writing)
    ISBN 978-0-472-07188-3 (cloth : acid-free paper) — ISBN 978-0-472-05188-5
(pbk. : acid-free paper)
    I. Title.
PS3562.E16H86   2012
814'.54—dc23   2012011046

For Zarko Paic and Marjan Strojan

Acknowledgments

"*Ars poetica*" first appeared in *What Will Suffice: Contemporary American Poets on the Art of Poetry* (ed. Christopher Buckley and Christopher Merrill, Gibbs-Smith Publishers, 1995); "... not a state of mind" first appeared in the *Mississippi Review* (vol. 19, no. 3, 1991); "Only connect . . ." appeared in *The Practice of Poetry* (ed. Robin Behn and Chase Twichell, HarperPerennial, 1992); "Making a Case; or, 'Where Are You Coming From?' " first appeared in *Writers on Writing* (ed. Robert Pack and Jay Parini, University Press of New England, 1991) and subsequently in *After Confession: Poetry as Autobiography* (ed. Kate Sontag and David Graham, Graywolf Press, 2001); "Either/and/Or; or, You're Not as Dumb as You Think" was presented as a lecture at the annual Teachers' Seminar, The Robert Frost Place (Franconia, N.H., 2004); "From Sublime to Rigamarole: Relations of Frost to Wordsworth" appeared in *Studies in Romanticism* (vol. 19, no. 1, 1980); "On Keats's 'To Autumn'" appeared in *Touchstones: American Poets on a Favorite Poem* (ed. Robert Pack and Jay Parini, University Press of New England, 1991); "Wordsworth and His 'Michael': The Pastor Passes" appeared in *ELH* (no. 45, 1978); "Fact, Dream, and Labor: Robert Frost and the New England Attitude" was published in the *Writers' Chronicle* (vol. 35, no. 2, 2002); "The Knife, a Parable" first appeared in the *Dublin Review* (Summer 2003); " 'I Recognize Thy Glory': On the American Nature Essay" appeared in the *Sewanee Review* (vol. 1, no. 3, 1998); " 'Fathomless: How a Poem Happens" appeared online at *Contemporary Poets Discuss the Making of Poems,* howapoemhappens.blogspot.com; "Mercy, Mercy, Mercy: A Poet's Awkwardness" was presented to MFA students at the University of North Carolina, Wilmington, in 2008; "To a Writer Just Starting: An Abcedarium" appeared in the *Writers' Chronicle* (vol. 30, no. 1, 2000); "On Bibliodiversity" was presented at the International P.E.N. Conference (Bled, Slovenia, 2011) and published as part of the proceedings; "Why I Believe" appeared in *Image* (no. 55, Fall 2007); my poem "Accident" was published in the *Floating Candles* (University of Illinois Press, 1982); my poems "A Hundred Himalayas" and "Hole" were published in *Ghost Pain* (Sarabande Books, 2005).

Contents

Preface: A Hundred Himalayas

I stop for breath at height of land—not much
at that, a loaflike clump, the likes of which

I'd have sneered at, younger. Forgive the body's failures,
I think, you've climbed a hundred Himalayas,

hill by hill in 60 years. My dog
must think it queer, that I should stop so long . . .

No, that's the sentimentalist, allusion-
monger. No thought in a dog, hence no confusion.

He does what he does, or rather, what I do.
Beast's obedience. And what have I to show

that's so much different? Which is not to say
I have peculiar reason to complain.

I don't. I'm standing here. Meanwhile one of my brothers
lies long since buried, and in this single winter

the Crab has clawed too many else to count.
"From the rising up of the sun to the going down,"

I've read, "The mighty God has called the world."
Indeed. Not mighty myself, I choose to hail

the things that are, like time, and death, and love.
Above all love. In a nearby stump, a groove

holds something shining: a perfect jewel of quartz—
purple, enduring, shaped somewhat like a heart.

The day's sufficient to the day. A simple stone . . .
I conquer my small Everests one by one.

23 April 2003

A Hundred Himalayas: Essays on Life
and Literature

The American fictionist Flannery O'Connor declared herself "an author congenitally innocent of theory, but with certain preoccupations."

It seems natural that O'Connor should be one of my heroes, and if I possessed her wit, I might say something equally bright of myself.

A Hundred Himalayas: I entitle this potpourri after a poem of mine, one that like these essays implies both the persistence of the preoccupations—which we might call lyrical—and the absence of any theory—which we might call epical.

If there is grandeur at all in this volume, then, it must come in small increments. Its speculations are akin to my having climbed a great series of New England hills, as I have, for even longer than the thirty years and some they represent: in such a process I hope to have found a certain elevation, without at any point taking on Everest-like challenges.

Mine are essays quasi-literary and quasi-philosophical, by an author quasi-provincial. I do not mean any false modesty by that self-description. I taught for decades, after all, at eminent institutions in America and abroad. I hold a PhD in comparative literature from Yale, a distinguished credential, at least on the face of it. And yet even as I pursued my studies toward that degree almost forty years ago, I knew I was not truly meant for a scholar nor for any sort of grand thinker.

During my time at Yale, the patriarchs of the New Criticism—W. K. Wimsatt, Frederick Pottle, Talbot Donaldson, Cleanth Brooks, and others—had lately been confronted by the young lions of literary theory. This meant in part that a fundamentally British- and Christian-derived academy was now besieged by a rather Continental, and in its brightest figures an emphatically Jewish, set of personalities and assumptions.

It was a heady period, in spite of, or more likely because of, its occasional contentiousness. In their own Olympian way, of course, the culture wars of late-'60s academic thought vaguely mirrored what was going on in the streets during that heyday of civil rights agitation, antiwar demonstration, sexual liberation, and general skepticism of the so-called American Dream.

My political instincts and actions back then (and in large measure today, however much older age may have mollified them) were entirely with the rebels. And yet, try as I might to learn the manner of the theorists, praising it to friend and foe alike, when it came to literary study, I was secretly a lot more comfortable with the old *explication de texte* mode of New Criticism than I was with structuralism, semiotics, deconstruction, and the rest.

Though my heritage is Irish on the one side and Mennonite German on the other, something in me seems to thrive on Anglo-American empiricism. If I can't see, hear, touch, taste, or feel something, at least in mind, then I'm unlikely to learn it. (Hence my virtual expulsion from every school and university course concerned with higher mathematics, for example.) What was once called practical criticism, therefore, is closer to my métier than a more rarefied approach.

It is small wonder that, even as I have remained in the academic world, I long ago turned to poetic utterance rather than intellectual, and cultivated many of my dearest associations among decidedly unbookish folk.

I have lived in upper New England all of my adult life. Yankee pragmatism attracts me. No surprise that my own favored genius should be the *genius loci* of this region, Robert Frost, nor that these essays so frequently touch on his work, even, I fear, to the point of reiterativeness.

It may be that I share with Frost a sort of *border* existence, occupying a territory that is not quite intellectual and not quite bumpkin. (Curiously, and maybe quite coincidentally, I've also long been *geographically* on the border of New Hampshire and Vermont, and close to the Canadian border.) Though I don't make the public effort that Frost did to disguise learning, still, like his, my learning is less crucial to me than other, more important impulses: that is, such erudition as I command comes *in support of* those impulses: my lust for the wild, natural world; my devotion to family life; my local friendships; even my odd and heterodox Christianity, which has made me a deacon and moderator in the local Congregational church (last house on the left, as my former pastor Susan Tarantino put it).

In a word, I am interested, as I've been since I first read Wordsworth's *Lyrical Ballads* at age fifteen, in how a sensibility, in my own case a poet's, may find sustenance and even song—in quotidian life among quotidian personalities, his own included. I have, for better or worse, imagined that my extended residence in postage-stamp-sized towns, where I know just about everybody, allows me to read the great issues of the world—life, death, love, hatred, character, ecology in all its meanings—in small script.

Such an inclination colors my regard for poetry, poets, indeed literature and writers in general. How could it not? Hence my similarly reiterative discourse on Wordsworth and on Keats, his self-acknowledged if unruly stepson.

In one way or another, I suspect that the following musings all circle around those "preoccupations" referred to by the great O'Connor and shared by my other literary heroes.

I.

Abecedarium

Ars poetica

⸙

ACCIDENT

Never to remember
New York City
Mingus's splendid tirades
Chico Max
the MJQ or early Gerry
he rides
his bike shooting out of woods like a switchblade
onto the lane
in our meadow where night air
leaves a slick on the gravel. This dawn
has no steam breathing through pavement cobbles
but a purple moth struggles
with the wet burden like Elvin
Jones in a gin-soaked club
and with his half-shucked shell
into such brief improvisation
of beauty that if the boy were nearer
or it were an hour later
(daytime frogs on the beat
like morning cops—Ninth at Broadway, dawn,
twenty years gone—
or my daughter doing her scat
voices drowning
the riff of wings like tiny high-hat cymbals)
I would never have noticed

The muted sun like Miles cuts through
the mistflumes' chorus
on the river where mayflies
lose their shifting hold on pebbles
at the bottom and make their way up
and trout at their stations hover like trebles
In the haysweet hills
the I I think I am
beats against the snare of the past

3

and sleep and dream
      Hard case
My son repeats
the terrible solo again
and again in his seventh summer
that decrescendo
dreaming his bike a flyer
set for the moon like Diz
Last night my baby daughter
poked a thumb at the ofay moon
and sang, "I want it." She thinks
it's Big Rock Candy. Meatfat and drink
clash in my sour intestines
like Monk's odd clusters at the old Half Note
The moth flies up
and clings in splendor to a screen

Hanging in country air
there's the boy's high wail
as his fender shivers like a tambourine

I've always been compelled—no matter its overuse, sometimes in bizarre ways—by Frost's notion of a poem as a "momentary stay against confusion." This is likely because I believe my existence would be a jumble without recourse to writing, especially the writing of poetry. Whatever their quality, my poems provide the means to discover otherwise unknowable connections among my soul's responses.

Like anyone, I'm bombarded by things, ideas, emotions, which arrive in no prevenient order or integrity. If they are to achieve any such shapeliness at all, it will be an essentially poetical one. For me, then, *ars poetica* must be *ars vitae* and vice-versa. To affirm, say, that I treasure my wife and children is to imagine my life with them as somehow an ongoing poem, this being my metaphor for every worthwhile thing I do (even the writing of fiction and nonfiction).

Therefore, while I've never set out to make a poem about poetry—in truth, despite the frequent exceptions of a Stevens or a Williams, such efforts often bore me—each of my poems is inevitably about being a poet, because that self-definition charges every relation to my surroundings: human, natural, and, since I call myself Christian, supernatural.

"Accident" is a case in point, and the first thing I should say about it, no matter the poem's seeming melancholy, is that I don't regard it as gloomy. I impute to it rather the spirit of a certain Wordsworth passage (never mind if it contradicts Frost's formula): "I could wish my days to be / Bound each to each by natural piety." My more specific nature po-ems aim especially to find that sort of continuity; but this one finds it too, at least partly. And—as is usually the case with my work, to my sat-isfaction—accidentally.

One August morning in 1979, I walked outdoors, passing first through my woodshed, where a gorgeous moth, numb with unseason-able cold, struggled to get airborne. The night before, a local radio show had played more than an hour's worth of Charles Mingus, and my head was yet full of his rhythms and melodies. I couldn't and still can't think of Mingus without wincing slightly to recall his public chastisement of my untimely applause, as he considered it, at a 1961 performance in the East Village, but, as a college student not far from New York back then, I kept going to hear the great man whenever I could.

My first son, like me an early riser, was just learning to ride a bicy-cle; as I looked out on the meadow where he practiced, it occurred to me that—reared in what was pretty much boondocks—he might never have so specifically urban a memory as that old one of mine, unless like me he went to an urban college.

I forgot all this, of course, as soon as he took his nasty spill. I did not, however, forget it long. The accident gripped my thoughts when I returned to my study. So, I discovered, did the early '60s New York jazz scene. The moth too. There was emotional stuff in each, and—as my *ars poetica,* to flatter it with the name, requires—I set about digging for what they had in common.

The very word *accident* proved quickly helpful. Pondering its Latin root (*accidens*), I surmised that, while listening years back to certain mu-sicians, I'd experienced beauties "falling toward" me. It helped also that "accidentals" were notes outside the key signature of a given composi-tion, of which notes there were of course plenty in Mingus-era jazz. It struck me that on this particular morning other beauties had likewise fallen, that they were forcing my soul out of its quotidian key (plain C major), and even its tempo (a stalwart 4/4).

All of a sudden the world had turned tuneful, and I felt oddly lucky. I registered mild sadness for the moth, like each of us so ephemeral, and more than that for Mingus, lately silenced by his deadly sclerosis, and of course for my slightly wounded son. Yet as I wrote I also felt blessed, above all to have chosen a poet's life, because if like anyone I'd often witnessed "brief improvisation[s] of beauty," I'd also been able, however imperfectly, to protract their span on the page.

And on this particular morning there had, as so often, been other luck too: I could have come outdoors through kitchen rather than woodshed; my boy could have been shooting baskets rather than riding a bike; had I listened not to a jazz show but to a Red Sox game the evening before, box scores rather than musical ones might have been on my mind.

I did feel real pathos in these things that had stopped me in my tracks, though I was just another man and father that morning. Any one of these phenomena might have reduced me to moping, especially the bicycle mishap, which as every parent will understand dramatized my child's plain, human vulnerability. The passage of time, our inevitable mortality, the very improvisatory quality of our lives all might simply have spun my brain; yet at least momentarily, I had the means to stay such prospective confusion.

In "Accident," "The I I think I am / beats against the snare of the past"; it fears discontinuity between now and then, not to mention between a father's experience and the experience of his flesh and blood, zooming so recklessly downhill on wobbly wheels.

Yet the poem at last seemed able to impose an integrity on pain, loss, joy, and beauty, to bind them each to each.

If the world plays quickly ahead from past to present, if it is rife with other disparities as well, there are moments when it proceeds somehow to harmony, and when even falling may seem an ascent. To record these instants seems at least a partial justification of my calling.

Either/and/Or; or, You're Not
as Dumb as You Think

✧

I START WITH A PREMISE that will make teaching poetry[1] seem even
more difficult than we suppose. Poetry's main mission is to move us out
of conventional thinking.

That is, most poetry since the nineteenth century has been a vehicle for the night mind, the passive mind, what we lately call the right
brain. But if poetry isn't chiefly a rational effort, how come we teach it
as if it were? That's the main issue I want to address.

For starters, what do we mean by conventional thinking? Our social
and intellectual lives as westerners are derived largely from the Enlightenment, which means that one of our conventional virtues is, precisely,
reason. The mind I speak of neither dismisses nor attacks reason; it
simply deprives it of primacy.

That mind challenges our hearty commitment to dialectic, to pat-
terns of either/or. I'm not complaining about the commitment, reason
serving us well in a great many ways, the lack of it often woefully afflict-
ing contemporary politics, for instance. Nor do I claim that right-brain
thinking is automatically preferable to left-brain. I maintain only that
the right brain needs nourishment: to starve it is to make for a more
general starvation, or at least that's so for artists.

We often hear that poems are transformative. The word can be
summoned too facilely, yet it can be accurate, and one goal for us as
teachers is to recognize such accuracy. If our students are genuinely
moved by what they read in verse, that may be because a successful
poem changes their visions. Here's a widely known work by James
Wright.

AUTUMN BEGINS IN MARTINS FERRY, OHIO

In the Shreve High football stadium,
I think of Polacks nursing long beers in Tiltonsville,
And gray faces of Negroes in the blast furnace at Benwood,
And the ruptured night watchman of Wheeling Steel,
Dreaming of heroes.

All the proud fathers are ashamed to go home.
Their women cluck like starved pullets,
Dying for love.

Therefore,
Their sons grow suicidally beautiful
At the beginning of October,
And gallop terribly against each other's bodies.

How would a conventional response to this poem look? *Thesis:* the fanatical attachment to high school athletics in America's small towns is a terrible thing. *Antithesis:* it's a good one. Either/Or. Those who dislike our national passion for sports might seem to have an edge here: they can argue that many a school system, unable to buy books for its courses, nonetheless manages to provide spanking uniforms and weight training rooms for its teams. But there may be something to the antithetical argument, that sports are a means of expression for kids who have precious few avenues to such expression.

Syllogistic thinking would lead us to *synthesis.* But the real issue here should be what *the poem* thinks. Which side is it on? If we answer that question too definitely, we have paid insufficient attention to its language; we've imported our own judgments. But even if synthetic thinking leads to mere compromise, I believe, it misses Wright's point.

Wright's last stanza does suggest that the football season involves inexcusable sacrifice: the boys "gallop terribly against each other's bodies." Preceding lines may further suggest that these young men are being used to rally the falling morale of their disenchanted parents:

All the proud fathers are ashamed to go home.
Their women cluck like starved pullets,
Dying for love.

Wright slyly invites us to imagine that the debate is over. His very next word is *Therefore.*

That word bodes a conclusion to either/or thinking, and so our partisans may bull right ahead to what, no doubt, they already believe, on the basis not of the poem but of other considerations. However much the false dialectic and the *Therefore* lead us to expect reductive conclusion, though, Wright's poem opens onto all manner of possibility.

I'll be talking in a moment about the necessity of encouraging our students to ask dumb questions, as they might name them. They mean—and they're inappropriately ashamed of it—that they wish they knew some plain facts, though they feel embarrassed to say so. I can't emphasize enough that we too ought to seek out these plain facts to the fullest degree possible before offering grander commentary.

Here's an example of a dumb question: *Where* does the poet experience the reflections we've just read about? That's easy: the very first line tells us that he's doing his thinking "In the Shreve High football stadium."

The poet's at the game. Unless he's there in some capacity akin to a war reporter's, don't the sidelines seem an odd place for one who considers the football culture a "terrible" thing? On the basis of so mundane a detail, things start to look a bit more complicated than we'd perhaps imagined. In our rush to conclusion, many of us may have overlooked a crucial detail, one that was right there in front of our noses.

I'm suggesting that before doing anything else, we must consider a poem's presentation at its most basic. Note, for example, how Wright points out not merely that the players grow suicidal in October; he describes them as suicidally *beautiful.* This very pair of words could trigger a fruitful sort of class discussion. The game of football can be ruinous and violent, no doubt; but it likewise can be a beautiful spectacle. Do the students agree? With what? Why? Why not? More difficult and more important a question, one that might well invite further interesting classroom response: Are violence and beauty in some way connected to one another? Why or why not? How? Is this always so?

I can discover no metaphorical language in "Autumn Comes to Martin's Ferry, Ohio." So any legitimate discussion will be based on the poem's literal words. And these will show that, within the poem itself, no exclusively right answer exists to the questions it provokes. The poem wants to register as many responses as possible, even if these be contradictory or confusing, as they no doubt are to the author.

Yes, poetry can be transformative at its best: it can change our clear-eyed, rational, opinionated responses into the sort of perception that allows a whole flock of balloons to stay in the air at once. The "right" answer to the questions raised by the poem under discussion may in one moment be that football and its boosterism are evil; in the next, that they are redemptive; most disturbingly, that all along they're *both at once.* The scene before us does not admit of simple settlement.

The aptness of Robert Frost's advice to the reader remains, however much our communications technology has changed: "If you want a message, call Western Union."

The impulse to message accounts for the fact that deliberately political poetry, for example, so often seems unpoetic, even, or maybe especially, if you agree with a given political poem's politics. The poem does not render an author's discovery of something novel and thus necessarily ambiguous so much as it illustrates his or her preexisting beliefs.

To that extent, there is no surprise recognition for the poet in the writing, so no sense in the *reader* of the author's startled realization. This is also why some of the most subversive and revolutionary poetry, like many of Blake's *Songs of Innocence,* seem on the surface to have no political aims at all: rather, in shaking up conventional wisdom (I think of the Judaean-liberationist Jesus's parables in the same light), they can't help but be politically volatile.

All this deprives us teachers of the premises we often rely on. That's less daunting for me, probably, than for you: while I'm safely communing with college kids who already more or less like poetry, or at least aren't averse to it, many of you as high school instructors are confronting a bunch of baggy pants and belly shirts and backward caps and pierced eyebrows. You're up against *attitude.* The attitude implies something to which poetry, if I'm right about its anti-conventionalism, ought justly to appeal, but more on that later.

I am aware of student expectations at all levels. Those who actually pay attention are often desperate for their teachers to know and to share "correct answers." They're uncomfortable with ambiguity, and why not? Doesn't ambiguity make you uncomfortable too? It does me; and so I have felt and too frequently yielded to the great temptation to reduce poetry, precisely, to the message that Frost sneered at.

At my most honest, though, I know I'm wrong to do that. I know full well that poetry does not ordinarily mean to put us at ease; it means to do the opposite, at least with regard to consecutive thinking. And so, if I do my job right, I know my students must at length see poetry as multifold, disturbing, fascinating. Even their beloved hip-hop, at its very best, will therefore seem formulaic, as indeed it usually is, compared.

When I'm having any success with my own poetry, I know that my mind has adequately resisted the either/or dialectic. And it's by pointing out the difference between what I've too often asked of a poem in English class and what I ask of it as a poet that I hope to say something about how that gap may be bridged.

I'll start by imagining myself not in a creative writing class, but rather in what many of my academic colleagues call a "straight" English class. (That adjective—*straight*—suggests that we artsy folk are bent or warped or whatever. I'll leave that to them.) In that conventional class, I'm likely to ask, "What does the poet want to tell us?" The question is silly, I think; but it can also be dangerous, in the manner of anything based on a half-truth. We may set off in hot pursuit of meaning, so hot that the other half is obscured. If *Paradise Lost,* to pick a momentous example, merely illustrates Milton's idea of free will, and does so only by glossing Old and New Testament texts, then the delicious sinuosity of Milton's verse may escape us, for example, as may his inclination, which William Blake first intuited, sometimes to favor the diabolical over the divine.

I'll come back to such matters as I go along.

Let me suggest one consequence of my commentary so far: when we teach poetry, we must dissolve another conventional either/or distinction: that of form and content, technique and subject matter. Technique for a poet is a crucial part of subject matter. A *vers libre* Horace, for example, would not be Horace at all; a prose poem by Emily Dickinson would be a creature we've never seen. The popular, free-verse "translations" of the great Sufi formalist Rumi by Coleman Barks, a writer innocent of the language he claims to render, must surely have little in common with the real Rumi, just as Alexander Pope's Shakespeare-in-couplets missed a world of achievement by the great bard himself. In his or her choice of *means* for a poem, a writer is in one way or another acting out the drama of its creation.

As Wallace Stevens once put it, "The poem is the cry of its occasion: / Not ideas about the thing but the thing itself." In some very profound way, a poem is a testimony to its own coming into being, to how an arrangement of words gave rise to further arrangements.

The most important thing I can say about how poems develop may be that poetry is a response to human discomfort. Something is going on in the writer's heart and soul that he or she can't quite figure out. A poem is thus an effort to get something into words that will both testify to the discomfort and transform it—that word again—into something shapely, though failure to achieve such shapeliness may turn out to be central to the poem's drama as well.

If the poet him- or herself feels ill at ease as he or she starts to write, what right have we to demand that we readers feel otherwise as we encounter the poem? What right have we, to echo myself, to regard any question as dumb? A student may ask, as I've urged, Where *are* we anyhow? By what right do we look on that question as trivial? Or maybe our reader is confused about point of view, an issue every bit as important in a lyric as in a story, and which is anything but a mere technical decision: by choosing this or that perspective, an author is saying something crucial about content.

When James Wright puts himself in the Shreve High football stadium, he not only establishes his own perspective but also makes it, at least *pro tempore,* that of his reader. When he uses the first person, the identity and character of the "I" have as much to do with what the poem's about as any other factor. Wright must ask himself, and he therefore asks us, What on earth am I doing in this place? Perspective in "Autumn Begins in Martin's Ferry, Ohio" is ultimately shifty, even blurry. To that extent, the poem's meaning remains a hard thing to pin down, which is very much part of its "meaning"—a grand part at that.

Archibald MacLeish famously declared that "a poem should not mean but be." Well, okay—but now what? We still have a class to conduct. Our response to a poem's being must therefore be more than "Oh wow, that's awesome," or "Oh wow, that stinks" or "This is all a jumble." There can be and must be some way or ways to a more penetrating response.

I'd like not so much to challenge as to extend MacLeish's dictum. We say that a poet wishes to move us, and we all wish our students would be moved. But I want to make use of that verb in a number of ways. Obviously, the poet wants us to experience emotion of some kind. And yet to do that, she or he must move us in an almost physical way, must take us from one world into another or others. In speaking of how the poet succeeds or fails, it may be helpful to think less of what a poet is saying than what he or she is *doing*.

So let me suggest that a poem must not mean but be . . . and do.

Okay again, but again, now what? Is this notion any more helpful than MacLeish's little koan? Well, I've found it so, if only because it further helps us to think of poetry less as a complex of intellectual specu-lations than as a unit of drama. To conceive of a poem's dramatic val-ues may help us among other things to overcome our own uncertainty, and more especially that of our students, as they approach a poem. How may it do that?

If students think that poetry is primarily full of thoughtful en-deavor, or if they have a notion of thought that is restrictedly ratiocina-tive, they'll worry that because they can't grasp the thoughts right away, they're dumb (that same damned adjective). If we begin with matters less abstract, elusive, hard to know, however, we may save them from that needless discomfiture.

So why not begin with what we *can* know? Why not ask the dumb questions ourselves? Here are some potentially helpful questions, which of course aren't dumb at all: Who is the protagonist? Why is he or she in this emotional, or even this physical circumstance? It may even be worthwhile, if we have anything to go on, to find out what he or she looks like, how old or young he or she is, how handsome or ugly. On and on. Such basics, not all, of course, applicable to everything we read, may have a real influence on the poem's dramatic trajectory. So does our an-swer to another supremely worthwhile dumb question: What happens?

In responding to a poem, it is altogether appropriate to summon the categories we often apply to a play, or even to conventional fiction: character, setting, and plot. These are not always relevant, no, but it's surprising how often they are. A poet includes such matters as a way of inviting us into her or his world. Or should, by my lights. (I say all this, by the way, in full recognition that there have been practitioners, at least since the Moderns, who dismiss all these concerns as naive. In the words of Scripture, they have their reward.)

To get at as many of these apparently literal matters as we can is essential to our reading. To get at them in a classroom setting is not only to forgive but to welcome our students' bumbling responses. As I've just said (and I'm being deliberately redundant), they should know that poetry itself is, at its heart, a working out of similar bumbling on the poet's part. What does James Wright feel at that suicidally beautiful football game if not such uncertainty?

The working out of uncertainty is what a poem "does," even if the result is no permanent resolution, any more than Cordelia's death fully resolves *King Lear*. If answers or resolutions to the poet's situation were obvious and sure, then he or she would have had small reason to choose poetry as a vehicle in the first place. Ambiguity is essential to what I'm saying. The heart of my argument is that good poems—like good plays—transcend the either/or. They live in the realm that Carl Jung described as "either *and* or."

Now none of what I have said so far means that conclusions, even ones derived from dialectical process, should be forgotten about entirely. Whether I'm being straight or warped, English teacher or poet, I must believe that when we read or teach or write about poetry, and when we ask our students to do the same, our intellectual expectations are not only legitimate but also valuable.

I, at least, wouldn't be much interested in any poetry that lacked ideas. A poet ought perhaps to know something about philosophy or anthropology or history or psychology or politics, and the more the better. It's only that, at its heart, his or her poetry is different from theory, and different from opinion of any kind. Or rather, as I should acknowledge with due humility, that much applies to poems that attract my own allegiance.

What, then, is this thing we call poetry? Well, sad to say, there's no better single definition of it than there is of painting or sculpture. Would Michelangelo, for instance, have considered Henry Moore a sculptor? Who knows? Would that fellow-radical Shelley have found poetry in Allen Ginsberg's "Howl"? Who knows? The definition of poetry has been fudged since before Homer. And I'll fudge it no less than the next Jack or Jill.

Some fudgings, however, are more equal than others: "Poetry," Robert Frost once said, "is what gets lost in translation." By that, I think, he means that if you were to "translate" his own work into a prose format, to be fanciful, you'd end up with a summary, exactly, of a great man's ideas, but, just as I suspect Mr. Barks loses a ton of what made Rumi Rumi, you'd lose what made Frost Frost.

Not that the New England bard's ideas weren't compelling. Of course they were, as his every letter and his every utterance about his art make clear. But truth to tell, the ideas in general were not often strikingly original. Neither were Dante's, for further example. Just as Shakespeare never made up a plot, Dante never made up his notions of Hell, Purgatory, Paradise, cultural history, or the shape of the human universe. Like my aspirant classroom poet, all these giants might have whined, "I don't have any ideas."

Of course, neither Frost nor Dante nor Shakespeare did whine about such a matter. Their lack of original ideas was hardly a problem, in fact, because what they did have, or hoped they had, was something much more valuable to an artist: ways of presenting their received ideas, ways that proved to be simply dazzling. As the fastidious Alexander Pope once insisted,

> True Art is Nature to advantage dressed,
> What oft was thought, but ne'er so well expressed.

As for me, I'll go on insisting that poetry, like any art, is concerned first and foremost with this matter of presentation, and of course for writers, presentation is as much concerned with language as music is concerned with notes, as painting is concerned with paint. Poetry, music, painting: each is first and foremost founded on the physical properties of its medium.

In the beginning was the Word, says the evangel John, and while I don't expect all readers and writers to share his Christianity, it's interesting to muse on that wisdom saying. What it says is that the Word makes the world. Mystical stuff, that, but so, often enough, is poetry. I do regard language rather mystically; I do look on the Word as powerfully creative. I do have literal faith in it.

Mind you, my faith in the Word's creative power does not mean for me that the use of fancy, frilly, "original" language will generate a poem, mine or anyone's. Sexy metaphor, clever rhyme, inventive meter: they won't cut it either, not on their own. We're not talking about decoration here. What we are talking about—or at least I am—is the fact that we English teachers are right, after all, to pose that question I mocked at the beginning of these thoughts: "What is the poet trying to say?"

I scarcely know every writer in America, but I do know hundreds.

And every one of them asks the very same question. That's what makes for the discomfort I've referred to. So what's the difference between what they ask and what is asked by me in my avatar as your English-class ogre? All I can say is something a bit fuzzy, which is that we writers put a slightly different spin on the question. We apply what could punningly be called a different English.

But back to real English, back at least to my own literature classes. In those classes, my students and I too frequently make a couple of mistakes.

1. We assume that the poet knew damned well what he or she wanted to say.
2. We assume that she or he just went right ahead and said it.

As poets, though, for better or worse, my writing students and I know something much different. We're trying to say something, all right; trouble is, we don't know just what that will turn out to be. Not at least when we make up our minds, from whatever irrational motive, to write a poem. No, as poets we just take a leap of faith. We jump into something. What?

Again, we don't high-dive into philosophy or theology, not into politics, not into any other sort of abstracter stuff. No. We jump into our materials—which is to say that we jump into the Word—which is to say we jump into language, which is to say that when we make that jump off the high board, we know we may take a belly-flop, and most of the time we probably will. But we also believe that if we're lucky (and what we call "inspiration" is often no more than being lucky), we may land on something that we can call a poem. At least for the moment.

What I've called the drama of a poem is very frequently the demonstration, in the poem, of how we landed there, how we came to our discoveries, how we grappled with our confusions.

The real problem of my self-styled idea-less student may very well have been that she or he didn't apply the right English to her poem. She misconstrued what any poem is trying to say. In my straight course, she gathered that poetry was all about concepts, and because she considered herself lacking in that department, she tried to dress up what few she did have, tried to put them into flowery or rhythmic language. And, just to prove she wasn't dumb, she slipped in a few things that she vaguely understood to be metaphors, because poets use those things, right? She ventured into alliteration and assonance; she loaded her poem with simile, that irresistible siren of the neophyte. Having done all this, she hoped to make a poem. Why didn't she?

Well, again, she failed to imagine that in the beginning was the Word, and therefore believed that all she had to do was cloak some opinions with the right "lyrical" trappings and she'd have an object we could call a poem.

None of that worked, and it never will. It can't.

Therefore did she tear her hair. Therefore did she scream: *This is really awful!* And she was right.

In my warped capacity as author, I'd tell her this, as I tell all of you interested in the writing of verse or in talking about it or teaching it: the biggest handicap to any poet, beginner or veteran, is that you are trying too mightily to take things you already know, write them down in whatever form, and then assume that you've had the Eureka experience. It's no go, alas, as I have empirically proved to myself after so many years in both my professional capacities.

But if I tell my fictive student to start writing about something or, just as often, someone that rattled her chains in some way, what do I mean? Well, let's imagine. She might be out walking, and she might come to a place where "Two roads diverged in a yellow wood." Good enough. I now urge her to put something down about that place in words. Because, however mystical my faith in the Word as I earlier described it, however mystical or spiritual that combination of words we call a poem may prove, one starts with the things of this world. One experiences his or her unsettledness among them. In recording that condition, one invites the reader into the poem. The invitation is an acknowledgment of the author's and reader's common ground. This much at least we can see and say: "Two roads diverged in a yellow wood." Now at least we have a dramatic setting.

"Knowing how way leads on to way," I think *I* know what that means. I believe that real immersion in any experience, any real effort to render that experience in language, can ideally lead a poet on to poetry. What sort of poetry? We don't and probably should not know. To possess foreknowledge may well be ruinous, may land the writer's experience in the dread domain of either/or, one or the other. Poets should avoid that neighborhood; it's a bad one.

NOTE

1. Delivered at the Robert Frost Place Conference on Poetry and Teaching, June 2006.

"Fathomless": How a Poem Happens

∞

FATHOMLESS

I remember that store, and the nasty redneck whose stink
seemed a challenge to everyone in it. The scene
is decades old, but I'm still confused that no one
took up the challenge—including me, though I liked
an occasional fight back then. The prospect of pain

meant less to me once, I guess. An aneurism
had just killed my brother, so the pain I'm talking about
was my body's. I breathed up another pain that day.
I checked the man's beat pickup. Why would he want them,
those skunks knee-deep in its bed? I left the lot

still more confused, my sweet retriever shivering
on the seat beside me. The godawful smell still clung
to the dog's wet coat, and my own. There'd be no more hikes
for us that morning: rain had arrived, bone-chilling.
If you killed a skunk, why would you keep the thing?

To kill some time, I stopped at The Jackpot View.
We've always called it that. Five mountaintops bled
into mists to my east in New Hampshire. The sudden squalls
spilled leaves on the woods-floor's pall of nondescript hue.
Now he was dead. Now my brother was dead.

I can't define any God, but only this morning,
I caught a whiff of road-killed skunk and thought
I could speak of Him or Her or It as surely
as I could tell you the slightest thing concerning
the man I'm remembering now, the one who shot

or trapped or clubbed those miserable reeking creatures.
The smallest enigmas we ever encounter remain
as hard to explain as all the epical ones.
I've failed for years to fathom the death of my brother;
but it's just as hard to understand why a scene

in an old Vermont store should linger like dead-skunk odor,
which if you've lately been tainted comes back to scent you

whenever a rain blows in—or like some pains
you may have thought you'd long since gotten over,
but which at some odd prompting come back to haunt you.

When was this poem composed? How did it start?

I look back into my "Draft Copies" folder, and see that I began the poem in May of '09 and got it to the "finished" version in March of 2010. It began in the way I suggest in stanza 5: "only this morning, I caught a whiff of road-killed skunk." I was just driving down to the village when I passed the road kill, and the odor—smell being the most suggestive of the senses, the least willed—I thought, as I had for many years off and on, about the guy who, strangely as strangely can be, had all those dead skunks in his truck. To recall that episode was to recall that it followed hard on the long-ago death of my younger brother. The poem at large ensued from that association.

How many revisions did this poem undergo? How much time elapsed between the first and final drafts?

That same folder shows twenty-four stabs at getting it right. This one is number twenty-five. To be sure, some of the changes from late draft to later were pretty minor, a word here, a phrase there, etc. And some revision involved *undoing* some over-revision. But that many drafts are not uncommon for me, nor, I suspect, for most writers.

Do you believe in inspiration? How much of this poem was "received" and how much was the result of sweat and tears?

What we call "inspiration" is for me really the operation of what Proust called involuntary memory. Certain experiences suddenly come back to me, one often having nothing, apparently, to do with the other. The poem is "about" what in fact they do have to do with each other, which has to be something. I mean, the one who made the associations after all—well, that was no one but me.

How did this poem arrive at its final form? Did you consciously employ any principles of technique?

I have no interest in the formalist/free-verse debate, because the fiercer it gets, the stupider. The formalists accuse the free-versers of sloppy thinking and craft, as if such a slur applied to Dr. Williams, say; the free-verse zealots accuse the formalists of being Establishment figures, as if *vers libre* were somehow something new, and hadn't itself been the Establishment mode for eighty years or so now.

That said, I am a formalist, period, even when it may be unobvious, when, for instance, I use eccentric accentual metrics or nonce forms. It seems obvious enough here: five-line stanzas, five-stress lines, and rhymes or slant rhymes in lines 1 and 4 and in lines 2 and 5. I wrote, as always, a very quick draft of what came at me. Then I fooled around with finding a common number of lines per stanza, and giving each one of those lines a fixed set of stresses. (I should interject that two of the meters, tetrameter or pentameter, come at me much more effortlessly than any free-verse mode, a fact that even I don't quite understand, though it may have something to do with my youthful enthusiasm, which lingers, for certain vernacular music.) Then I noticed that lines 2 and 5 rhymed, or sort of, in one of the stanzas, and I fiddled around with making that true of them all. Ditto, with some tweakings, 1 and 4. And so on. Mere monkeying around.

For me, that sort of monkeying is a way of engaging in play, and submitting to what are sometimes called, more than a bit fuzzily, the musical properties of language, but above all of getting over any too willful effort to signify something. For me anyhow, this non-method allows the language and the formalities to lead me by the nose, as it were; I just tag along wherever they take me—sometimes to a poem, sometimes to an essay or, more rarely, a story, most frequently to a mess. But I take the ride in any case. I can't know if I've got something lively until I *have* taken the ride.

How long after you finished this poem did it first appear in print?

Without looking the matter up, I'd guess eighteen months.

How long do you let a poem "sit" before you send it off into the world? Do you have any rules about this or does your practice vary with every poem?

That varies with every poem. Usually I revise sporadically for a long, long time, leaving the poem in Desk Drawer Land for considerable spells between revisions. But all of us know that there is, now and then, the poem that arrives at no apparent cost to our energies. This is the Muses' way of rewarding us for all the hours we devote to the ones that come a lot harder. "Fathomless" belongs to the harder category.

Could you talk about fact and fiction and how this poem negotiates the two?

Everything in "Fathomless" is fact, or at least that's true—to use circular logic—of the factual parts. If I say in a poem that I lost a brother, for instance, that had better be verifiable. Same with that eccentric skunk-killer. I don't think this is a moral stance, though I do feel some unease when people fake experience, especially by way of making themselves look admirable or (God help us) sensitive. No, it's not so much a moral stance as one that enables me.

I am, I guess, a capital-R Realist Poet, to use a reductive label.

Is this a narrative poem?

It does tell a story, so maybe yes. That's not its only effort, of course, yet I do tend to think of myself as a poet who, no matter what he addresses, will have an interest if not necessarily in plot, then in other narrative concerns: character, setting, that sort of thing.

Do you remember whom you were reading when you wrote this poem? Any influences you'd care to disclose?

I can't recall what I may have been reading. My principal influences are nineteenth-century ones, especially Wordsworth and Keats. My principal American influence is Frost, though—not at all patently—Dickinson must be in there somehow too. More recent influences are, again, quite different poets, and I take different things from each, perhaps: Robert Penn Warren, Walcott, Bishop, Justice, and no doubt others whose effects may not be obvious even to me.

Do you have any particular audience in mind when you write, an ideal reader?

Yes, the reader whom I envision is sometimes one neighbor, sometimes a composite of several. These are people—crusty, feisty, laconic, and sometimes even xenophobic northern New England hill farm or lumberjack stock, or what's left of it—quite a few of whom are valued friends, though they'll never read a word of mine, unless maybe something in prose. Again, to picture these neighbors as I start to write is a trick that enables me; it makes no sense on earth.

Did you let anyone see drafts of this poem before you finished it? Is there an individual or a group of individuals with whom you regularly share work?

My wife knows me better than anyone, so she's in many respects my best critic. Above all, she can check me when I am faking it, maybe even trying to make myself look "sensitive" in that odious way. She is brilliant and literate, but it's important to me that she is not liter*ary*. I tease her that she's a recovering lawyer; in fact, she's a professional mediator. One of my favorite poets and friends, Fleda Brown, also sees almost all I do; so does Stephen Arkin, who's not a poet (he taught literature for four decades at San Francisco State and has remained one of my closest friends since we went to grad school together): but Steve is exquisitely attuned to language and is another keep-him-honest reader, knowing me as thoroughly as he does. I like these people to call me, especially, on any bullshit, any "poetic" posturing.

How does this poem differ from other poems of yours?

I'm not the one to judge that.

What is American about this poem?

Well, it is set in America, for starters. And, despite its formalism, it seeks to sound like actual speech, which is a very American concern. My dear friend Marjan Strojan, a Slovenian poet and my translator into his language, informs me for example that it's not a consideration at all among his compatriots.

Was this poem finished or abandoned?

Valéry was right about that. I got it as good as it was going to get, given such gifts as I own. Then I moved elsewhere.

"... not a state of mind"

First, some surmises about my assignment[1] here:

1. "It has sometimes been said" (passive voice) "that contemporary poetry, however technically brilliant" (demure subordinate clause), . . . and so on. Our editor, a thoroughly decent person, words her premise so as not to seem officious or arrogant. Still, I suspect she may want to make a more assertive statement: Our poets are long on razzle-dazzle, short on substance.

2. But she means poets born after 1935 or so, right? She doesn't expect us to chastise a Rich or Hecht or Levertov or Walcott or Carruth, whose finest works contain, in spades, all the qualities she alludes to.

3. The editor hopes her contributors will rebut or support those who blame the MFA explosion for our poetry's allegedly lamentable condition. Donald Hall is their captain, I guess, and a fairly formidable one, though oddly inclined to visit with and to address the despised MFAers and to cash their checks.

On to some of my responses:

1. Have the poets of *any* literary epoch had some collective vision, and so served up a unified statement? Have they ever like-mindedly understood what it meant—I use Mr. Hall's favorite word—to be ambitious? Consider the Romantics. I'd make a better case for "visionary" commonalty between Blake's *The Four Zoas* and Pope's *Dunciad,* say, than I would between the *Zoas* and Keats's "To Autumn." But I'd make a better case for "To Autumn"'s ambition than for *Don Juan's.* Etc. Generalizations about periods or movements attain validity, if ever, after a big chunk of time, and we should see our own (including postmodern, L-A-N-G-U-A-G-E, neo-formal, neo-narrative, et al.) as provisory and probably purblind, like the evaluative judgments they frequently imply, including *ambitious* or *technically brilliant,* let alone *great.*

2. Speaking of generality, who says we're surrounded by technical stars? However much he or she rants about others' formal or prosodic sloppiness, I rarely read a so-called New Formal-

ist, for example, whose own mastery in these respects simply knocks me out. R. S. Gwynn comes close, and more, I admit.) Indeed, if I myself had to make a statement, it would be that a great deal of free and regular verse alike in our time shows as much technical as visionary poverty.

Of course the distinction itself is impoverishing. Technique in the best poems is never a mere means to subject matter but a crucial *component* of subject matter. The way the speaker talks his way through the most complex portions, say, of "The Want Bone" is not "as important as Robert Pinsky's thoughts": it *is* his thoughts, in action, like Dante's—his gorgeous *ottava rima* resonant—in the *Comedy,* to choose a less than modest analogy.

Poetry, as my late friend Bill Matthews once quipped, is not criticism in reverse. Amen. A poem isn't some philosophical idea on the author's part, which she or he disguises by things like syntax or rhyme or meter or form or metaphor, things that we readers and critics in turn must jettison in order to arrive at his or her "meanings." English teachers may think so; we writers better not.

3. But most of us writers nowadays *are* English teachers, which is what leads many, not all of them outside the academy themselves, to blame The Sorry State of Poetry on its academic affiliation. Facile, I think. And premature: after all, we have about as much distance on the birth of our first MFA program as we do on *The Waste Land,* whose influence even someone as acute as William Carlos Williams could charge with all the deficiencies of his contemporaries' verse. Surely we should avoid similar overstatement with regard to the workshop: the poetry MFA is just too young to invite comfortable conclusions concerning its good or ill effects on our culture. With all respect to Hall, neither he nor we will know for certain in our lifetimes whether there's such a thing as a McPoem in the '90s. To be sure, there probably is . . . as there always was, well before anyone ever heard of Iowa or the Associated Writers' Programs.

4. For argument's sake, however, let's all agree that beneath our razzamatazz there is nothing but a great big Blah. What'll we do about that? Shall we sit down and choose to have a "vision" or make a "statement"? Can anyone truly believe in the feasibility of such an enterprise?

Likewise for ambition. In his spoken introduction to the marvelous *Live in New York* album, the late Cannonball Adderley said: "Hipness is not a state of mind; it's a fact of life. You don't *decide* you're hip. It just happens that way." For "hipness" and "hip," read "ambition" and "ambitious," and you'll catch my drift.

Our only genuine choice, it seems to me, is to do what we've always done at our best: summon as many resources—intellectual, spiritual, technical, visionary—as we can in all our poems. Then leave it to Time, that greatest anthologist, to sort our successes and failures.

NOTE

1. Written in response to a survey sent out by Angela Ball, editor of the *Mississippi Review,* as follows: "It has sometimes been said that contemporary poetry, however technically brilliant, lacks statement or vision. Please comment."

"Only connect . . ."

⌒∞⌒

WHETHER OR NOT A STUDENT ENDS UP a "formalist," she or he will (or should) want to know as much about the technical properties of poetry as possible. So as a poetry coach I have given a fair number of formal exercises over the years. My slant on these being insufficiently witty or bright, I won't catalog them here. Apart from those, I offer only one:

> *Select three entries from your journal, no two dated within four days of each other, and discover in verse the connection among them.*

I don't assign such an exercise, obviously, until after a few weeks of classes have gone by, and I assign it only once. Then I let it hover in the semester's atmosphere.

Truth is, I'm skeptical of exercises, which can too easily be understood as tricks, and although writing may contain one's personal tricks, it had better not *consist* of them, or not of them exclusively.

On the 6th of May, you saw two dogs locked in their procreative act, the larger female dragging the male around by his member; on the 10th, you broke your toe; on the 14th, it snowed out of season. Okay: go for it.

A premise: Most writers write, at least in some measure, to find out what their current obsessions are. Writing reveals these concerns, which may well previously have remained obscure to those writers themselves.

A problem: Most undergraduates have been (mis)educated into believing that literature's aims are abstract, intellectual, or philosophic; thus their greatest block is (quote) "I couldn't come up with an idea." Dogs, snow, toes: huh?

A remedy: "Couldn't come up with an 'idea'?" Well, good! Fully formed aprioristic notions will rob your writing of its potential vigor. My exercise, accordingly, should liberate students from the merely ideational into material more properly their own: personal idiom, for starters, and a whole range of as yet unarticulated responses to . . . Life.

In their required journals, they have entered things that arrested their attention. I trust that at my urging they have recorded these things with minimal editorializing or reflection. The three entries on which they'll base the assigned poem are well removed from one another precisely so that we won't get a bossy idea, packaged and summarized. For isn't the prime defect in most beginning verse its yen to report on experience, rather than artfully to suggest the mind/heart in the very process of experiencing?

Reprise—problem and remedy: Many academic instructors ask, What is the poet trying to say? As if she or he had some awful throat disease. The poet who successfully completes the above exercise may answer that what she or he is saying is what has been said. (Of course, it ought to make some sense: see Final Note.) The capital-M meaning of the poem, that is, resides exactly in the language, imagination, and logic that found the connections.

Our author simply and rightly supposes that, since she or he is the one to have made these three vivid observations, perhaps the more disparate the better, there *must* be a connection among them, and the poem that discovers them is its own meaningful gesture.

The point, I'll repeat, is to get the creative capacities off scratch, to prevent a poem's progress from being too strenuously willed; even though "ideas" inevitably emerge from one's poetry, they must not determine it.

Final note: Lest all this sound too awfully late-'60s or vulgar-Romantic, I should add that I place great emphasis on the intellect in verse. How could one read Spenser, say, or Louise Gluck, and not? But I stress too that intellectual control of a poem is something to apply *after* the materials have been allowed to float to the surface, as I hope my exercise may help them do.

II.

Making a Case

"I Recognize Thy Glory"
The American Nature Essay

෴

NATURE, AS COMMONLY UNDERSTOOD by the greatest writers in the genre under discussion, stands apart from all that is made or artificial, so that the "nature essay" is a contradiction in terms—and knows it.

I speak of the American nature essay, and more specifically of what I think its most interesting mode, whose practitioners descend from Thoreau and might include Aldo Leopold, say, or Edward Abbey, Gretel Ehrlich, Barry Lopez, James Kilgo, Rick Bass, or, in her best book, *Pilgrim at Tinker Creek,* Annie Dillard. Though neat distinctions are always suspect, I ignore what seems the more European, and particularly British, tradition of rural writing, whose contemporary practitioners might include the likes of Noel Perrin or Wendell Berry, writers who shun the volatile city in order to witness what they view as more harmonious—and even, as in writings on the harvest, more ritualized—human relations.

By contrast, Thoreauvian authors consider the development of most human relations, ritual or otherwise, to be a perversion of their longed-for, Emersonian "original relation" to nonhuman nature. I quote the scholar Peter Fritzell, from whose brilliant and encyclopedic *Nature Writing and America*[1] I have borrowed to the point of near plagiarism in parts of what follows:

> The most conspicuous trait of American nature writing is its narrator, the prototypical "I" of so much American literature, an Ishmael-like figure ranging the gamut of philosophical stances and psychological states, constantly (and unpredictably) shifting its point of view . . . , continually changing its tenses, its vocabulary, and its stylistic techniques—in almost every way indicating both the basic instability of its positions or perspectives and its final reluctance to bring conventional, "civilized" order to an experience best lived and understood in a continual series of situational surprises or unanticipated discoveries.

Fritzell implies that the nature essay is far closer to canonical American poetry than to anything else, and he quotes for example a famous passage from Abbey's *Desert Solitaire:*

Standing there, gaping at this monstrous and inhuman spectacle of rock and cloud and sky and space, I feel a ridiculous greed and possessiveness come over me. I want to know it all, possess it all, embrace the entire scene intimately, deeply, totally, as a man desires a beautiful woman. An insane wish? Perhaps not—at least there's nothing else, no one human, to dispute possession with me.

. . . Near the first group of arches, looming over a bend in the road, is a balanced rock about fifty feet high, mounted on a pedestal of equal height; it looks like a head from Easter Island, a stone god or a petrified ogre.

Abbey

Like a god, like an ogre? The personification of the natural is exactly the tendency I wish to suppress in myself, to eliminate for good. I am here not only to evade for a while the clamor and filth and confusion of the cultural apparatus but also to confront, immediately and directly if possible, the bare bones of existence, the elemental and fundamental, the bedrock which sustains us. I want to be able to look at and into a juniper tree, a piece of quartz, a spider, a vulture, and see it as it is in itself, devoid of all humanly ascribed qualities, anti-Kantian, even the categories of scientific description. To meet God or Medusa face to face, even if it means risking everything human in myself. I dream of a hard and brutal mysticism in which the naked self merges with a non-human world and yet somehow survives still intact, individual, separate. Paradox and bedrock.

The voice here seems exactly that of Fritzell's "prototypical figure in American nature writing," who feels within himself the painful clash of nature and culture, his very craft being a manifestation of the apparatus he longs to escape. Language and writing themselves, especially lyrical language and writing, are fabrications at variance with that abiding American desire to merge the self with something utterly other.

This brings me back to the nature essay as contradiction in terms: its authors passionately want it to be about nature, but it turns out really, and often maddeningly, to be about their own perceptions of nature, and thus finally about their self-perceptions. In *Pilgrim at Tinker Creek* you now and then hear the narrator resort to hard-scientific terminology. In *Walden* the "I" here and there catalogs weather, weights, and measures. I could go on, but mean mainly to say that in the nature essay, while the narrator occasionally seeks absolute clarity and factuality, he or she does so with immediate skepticism: such civilized modes of responding to quintessential nature can't be right, can they? And so the speaker falls into extreme self-consciousness and even self-irony. And yet it is from such an uncomfortable state that the best writing in his or her work emerges.

I can put such matters personally, if crudely. Anyone who spends as much time, especially alone, as I spend in woods and on waters must surmise the inutility of language. I cannot even here present the sort of experience to which words are inadequate, because I have to use words. "Tamarack." "Raven." "Eft." "Doe." "Granite." "Spawning bed." "The." "And." "Because."

And yet isn't the same dilemma encountered by anyone who spends a lot of time, especially alone, among deep feelings and who likewise wants to speak about that experience? As both essayist and poet, then, I think I share Edward Abbey's desire to witness the profoundest importances of my life in an unmediated way, to feel the dissolution of my separate self, and a simultaneous desire to hang onto that self so that I may testify to whatever I may chance upon.

To put my argument tersely: the lyric poet's aspirations always involve some merger of words and fundamentals, of language and the unutterable, and in this respect they resemble those of the nature essayist. Whatever his or her context or subject, the poet's ambitions are founded on the very paradox that Abbey limns in the paragraphs I cited: formulated language is an instant compromise of a subject's genuineness, an instant venture into artifice. That paradox, as he says, is unavoidable, basic: "bedrock."

It is not news that the cry against "mere art" is more persistent in American poetics than in other nations'. Always and everywhere, it seems, we hear the demand for our poems to be—what? Why, "natural," of course. Listen to poet-critic Jonathan Holden on this issue. After quoting a poem by Sandra McPherson, he likens it to "much contemporary poetry—particularly the kind being fostered in university creative-writing programs—a 'poetry of sensibility,' a cultivated attempt to imitate spontaneous vision, to produce through carefully muted craft the illusion of urgency."[2]

This commentator describes what we have, then, as a poetry of "affected naturalness." How's that for paradox? I do not mean, however, any more than Holden does, to condescend to McPherson or any other writer: the conflict between the literary and the natural is in some sense absolute, after all, so perhaps our clumsier efforts at denying that actuality, or even our defter ones, may be justified.

Such denial, you see, is basic to literary art, at least in the genres that lean least heavily on reason, and we undertake it in the clear knowledge that the best of our denials can never be more than half-successful. This is likely why we write so *many* poems and essays, though the motive might apply to all the other modes of imaginative writing. The single avenue I know to half-success begins— as I've noted before and will again—with our temporarily throwing aside the very issues of "craft," of "cultivation," and, emphatically, of "meaning."

Though I scarcely believe good writing in any genre is of necessity anti-rational, in the two I'm considering here, the lyric poem and the Thoreauvian essay, there is at least a great deal of non-rational energy. Or there ought to be, I'd claim, if either is going to catch a reader's attention. Consider Rick Bass's *The Nine Mile Wolves*.[3] At the very start, in a page or so of marvelously evocative prose, the author imagines those Montana wolves pulling down a quarry; and then come some telling afterthoughts:

> I can say what I want to say. I gave up my science badge a long time ago. . . .

> The story's so rich. I can begin anywhere.

> I can start with prey, which is what controls wolf numbers (not the other way around), or with history, which is rich in sin, cruelty, sensationalism (poisonings, maimings, torture). You can start with biology, or politics, or you can start with family, with loyalty, and even with the mystic-tinged edges of fate, which is where I choose to begin. It's all going to come together anyway. It has to. We're all following the wolf. To pretend anything else—to pretend that we are protecting the wolf, for instance, or managing him—is nonsense of the kind of immense proportions of which only our species is capable.

Bass, I would argue, is capable of prose that's as lyrical as any verse. And I'd argue that his own lyricism depends on his willingness to abandon himself to the primitive instincts of the animal self and, in apparent contradiction, to the primitive urge to speak. Neither of these urges conforms to an elaborate agenda, but only to its own hunger. Indeed, *agenda* is the very sort of notion each avoids like a trap.

Both self and speech assume a coherence in the world, but neither assumes it will be discovered in a logical way. (A different sort of inquiry from this would consider the inevitably sinuous, heavily subordinated syntax of the nature essay.) Like a predator on the scent, or like the most truly adept human hunter, the author follows signs that are at once cryptic and potentially eloquent. It is only the very act of pursuit that at length will lead to the connections among these signs.

I'm beginning to tend, almost perforce, toward some mystic-tinged edges myself, and toward abstraction. Let me once again try, therefore, to root my observations in personal experience. A typical nature essay will begin for me in the same manner as a typical poem. I'm speaking here not only of aesthetics or technique but also of far more literal matters, such as my inclination to hike long distances in the woods by myself, seeking not to think up subjects but to let my mind float free until, over time, perhaps over a dozen hikes or even years, I find that certain things have lodged themselves in my consciousness and now demand meditation, that they have "subjected" *me*.

In my volume *Hunting the Whole Way Home*,[4] there's an essay called "On the Bubble" which originally appeared in the special nature issue of the *Georgia Review* (Spring '93). Here is how it starts:

> Early June of 1992, below Stonehouse Mountain, Grafton County, New Hampshire—a place and time in which snow squalls, routine enough just weeks ago, will at last deserve the name freakish. In freshet beds where waters flared and vanished, frail shoots of jewelweed declare themselves; grass bursts the voles' winter tunnels; geese trail the Connecticut northward; the buck deer's antlers are in velvet; the woodchuck's busy to double in weight; trout sip the ponds' ephemerids; everywhere, the lovesick insistence of birds.

> Our family has lived ten years on this foothill's flank, but soon after dawn this morning—beckoned by the full day ahead—I hiked down from its mild summit for perhaps the last time. The ramble, especially under such circumstances, brought back the many I'd made there, in company or alone, one recollection summoning another, and that one still another, till outward prospects opened onto vaster, more labyrinthine inward views.

Yet that, in all honesty, is a paragraph I wrote late in the construction of this piece, after I happened on what, to use a simplism, the essay was about. The way it began conceptually was in my somehow remembering a beautiful, brown-phase fisher, who almost stepped across my toes one fall while I was deer-hunting; that, and the fact that, at the time I began feeling an itch to write this particular chapter, my family found itself on the point of moving from Stonehouse Mountain, which a speculator was planning to ruin; that, and the memory of my son blowing bubbles one spring morning at the top of the same little mountain.

These were things that, although removed from one another in a variety of ways, had lodged themselves in my heart and head. My essay began, then, in the spirit of Rick Bass: "It's all going to come together anyway. It has to."

Or maybe I began in the spirit of Wallace Stevens, in the sense that my essay was what he called "the poem of the mind in the act of finding what will suffice," *finding* and *mind* being the words I'd stress, for total sufficiency will always escape us. As I said early on, the nature essay turns out to be about the essayist's perception of nature, and thus about his or her mind's perception of itself.

This cannot and must not, however, be a static perception but one that unfolds in the very process of writing either essay or poem: it is an act, or rather multiple acts, of finding. To recall the words of Peter Fritzell to which I referred at the outset, the so-called nature essay seeks, however vainly and illogically, to replicate "experience best lived and understood in a continual series of situational surprises or unanticipated discoveries."

In this the nature essay is like a poem, because in either case it turns out that even our own minds are things we must find, and, at least in my experience, both the frustrations and the joys of poem or essay are intimately linked with that fact. When I say in the piece just quoted that "outward prospects opened onto vaster, more labyrinthine inward views," I am at once dismayed and exhilarated.

Like an Edward Abbey, I too would like now and then to immerse myself entirely and exclusively in outward prospects, a desire doomed to failure because, like him, I use language even when I'm silent. After all, I'm a writer. But yes, there is clearly elation in such a calling. Why else would one *be* a writer?

I'm also the sort of writer who derives profound pleasure from his sensibility's capacity to forge links in that non-rational, non-logical fashion I earlier indicated. I had not known, to recall my example, that a big brown weasel and my son's bubble-blowing had anything to do with one another, or with my reaction to the so-called development of our home mountain. To learn that they did connect was revealing and oddly thrilling.

And yet I cannot end just here, for fear of seeming to advocate, in poetry or prose, the virtues of utter self-regard. Which of us doesn't tire pretty easily of poems and essays founded on the belief that the least whiff of feeling on the author's part must interest his or her reader?

It's partly to save myself from such delusion that I am a passionate amateur naturalist. Yes, I may have opined that the ultimate subject of any American lyric or any American nature essay is the self's perception of the self, but at the risk of circular logic I'll also suggest that the lyric poet or essayist can be saved from mere narcissism by his or her immersion in subjects *outside* the self, especially ones that prove resistant to the individual human will, or at least the will's lust to heap meanings upon them. Such willful insistency, you see, is in my opinion the great enemy of what we call creativity; it is the faculty that works up an agenda.

A virtue of the natural world is, precisely, that it forever escapes all rigid agenda of the mind or will. In this regard, it can serve as a model. As such, the natural world has some further virtues as well, one of them being that an essay about it, a nature essay, demands accuracy. Fakery will wreck it. Indeed, one of the prime foibles I have noticed, for example, in undergraduates who want to write on nature, is that they like the idea of being green, but are green in quite another way. They are as apt, for instance, to put osage oranges in northern Vermont as hop hornbeam, anhingas on Lake Ontario as goldeneyes, and so on.

Yes, "the mind in the act of finding what will suffice" may be as much the final subject of a nature essay as of a poem, but that essay can't just say any old thing that occurs to it. It must establish its authority. The connections among its things and thoughts and emotions may and should be non-rational, but that's a long way from saying that its facts are finally irrelevant.

The factual fascinations of a Thoreau or a Dillard or a Barry Lopez represent some measure of self-defense, but they also provide appropriate ballast to essays that might otherwise be so self-conscious as to become utterly private and thus unpersuasive. If we speak only of our emotional workings, we exclude the reader. Likewise, if we don't know one tree, one bird, one rock, one fish, one animal from another, how seriously can our "love" for all these be taken?

In this regard, too, the demands of the nature essay seem models for the lyric poem. If I hear even so eminent a poet as Donald Hall, for instance, describe how "quail scream in the maw of the fisher" in his adoptive New Hampshire, I'm a little disinclined to listen to him on less factual subjects, there being no wild quail in that state at all. Brendan Galvin, in an excellent essay on nature and contemporary poetry in that same *Georgia Review* nature issue, makes a similar point after reading Gerald Stern's claim to have once been awakened by "two or three daws" in West Virginia, and the late Larry Levis's report on some Missouri linnets.

Galvin aptly quotes Robert Graves in this connection: "Fact is not truth, but a poet who willfully defies fact cannot achieve truth." The same, I would claim, for the poet who is ignorant of the facts on which she or he purports to found insight.

In our time, and the tendency is commendable enough, many an aspirant writer wants to speak on behalf of the natural world. To every such aspirant I've coached, however, I've stressed the importance of a sort of homework, though in the case of the nature essay the term is at best inexact. But whatever the genre, I'd argue, let it involve something Out There, and let the would-be renderer of that externality learn as much about it as he or she can. For all of us to concentrate, to the distressingly small extent we possibly can, on the Out-There may be the very discipline to deliver us, unexpectedly, into the realm of imagination in its least solipsistic typology.

I'll say that that sort of imagination is glorious, an adjective which intentionally echoes a passage by the great "nature poet" William Wordsworth at a sublime turn in *The Prelude*. The reader will encounter it elsewhere among my references, so vividly have the lines impressed themselves on my soul.

On a grand walking tour, the young Wordsworth, completely rapt in his observations of the French Alps, fails at one point to notice that he has crossed them. He describes his feelings after inquiring and being informed that the Simplon Pass now lies behind him:

> Imagination! Here the power so called
> Through sad incompetence of human speech,
> That awful power rose from the mind's abyss
> Like an unfathered vapour that enwraps,
> At once, some lonely traveler. I was lost;
> Halted without an effort to break through.

Years later, however, he understands something:

> But to my conscious soul I now can say,
> "I recognize thy glory. . . ."

No, nature doesn't "do" essays or poems. It exists in a way that quite specifically frustrates essays and poems, dramatizing as it does the "sad incompetence of human speech"; but in that very frustration, it may free up "awful powers" within us, ones that have lain undiscovered until the very moment we find them. To speak of them may, in some philosophic sense, be a come-down, a recognition of relative incompetence.

But we have to keep on trying. It's what, as writers, we do.

NOTES

1. Peter Fritzell, *Nature Writing and America: Essays upon a Cultural Type* (Ames: Iowa State University Press, 1990). Fritzell's is a book that cannot be overpraised for the richness of its argument and the equal wealth of its references

2. Jonathan Holden, *The Rhetoric of the Contemporary Lyric* (Bloomington: Indiana University Press, 1980).

3. Rick Bass, *The Nine Mile Wolves* (New York: Ballantine Books, 1992).

4. Sydney Lea, *Hunting the Whole Way Home* (Hanover and London: University Press of New England, 1994).

Mercy, Mercy, Mercy
A Poet's Awkwardness

⟨✦⟩

THIS PRESENTATION,[1] WHATEVER ITS WORTH, has turned out to be more confessional than I would have predicted. It begins with my meditating on the small knot that formed in my stomach when I was told today's audience would expect a craft talk. I've spoken, if anything, too much in public; why, then, this little spasm of nerves?

Well, yes, I've talked my share about the literary life, but have tended to shy away from that word *craft*. My unease, it occurs to me, may be derived from a time when I was your age or younger. My college offered no writing courses, and, like most old-style academics, my professors preferred their poets dead. And they'd have scoffed at communal discussion of poetic craft. Despite the career path I chose, based exactly on such conversation, maybe I carry a trace of their attitudes.

In any case, I was never versed in the patois I associate with a craft talk, and am hardly more at home with it even now. I could speak a lot more authoritatively on managing a New England woodlot or on how to train pointing dogs or what goes into editing a literary journal. I have lived for poetry, true, but not for poetry exclusively.

As an instructor, I don't think I've done any harm in the classroom, even though I don't speak MFA very well. And don't mistake me as bragging about my lack of an MFA or any formal creative writing credential at all. It would be absurd to bash the very courses I've taught for so long, and with such pleasure. It's only that I am tentative about exerting aesthetic authority, and rather suspicious of those who feel comfortable in doing so. It seems to me that too many craft discussions present a given speaker's personal approach as the proper one, trivializing or chastising other modes. The world would be the better for a little more humility than one notices in most quarters, including the literary.

Moreover, I have eclectic tastes. In valuing the best of Anthony Hecht, say, I feel no need to devalue that of Allen Ginsberg: in loving Frost, I needn't shun Moore; and so on. Clearly, when it comes to established poets, I am anything but doctrinaire in my tastes. Why should I be different in dealing with undergraduates and graduate students? I'd rather look at their poetry, if I can, in *its* imaginative terms than in those of my own writing. I have no brighter approach to pedagogy, then, than this: Let me see what you have done, and let me help you, if I'm able, to get out of your own way, to help your draft fulfill its own ambitions. The great architect Louis Kahn hoped his students at the University of Pennsylvania could learn to recognize what a building wanted to be; I hope the same for student poetry.

In brief, I'm suspicious of talks or essays or books that say, fundamentally, Here's How You Do It. Some thirty years ago, for instance, nervous as a cat about teaching my first creative writing course, I sought help from a volume called—or probably not, but something akin—*How to Write Fiction*. Oddly, I seemed undistracted by the fact that the author's own fiction had never much been published: at least I for one had never heard of any at that time, and I haven't since.

When I tried to apply the book's admonitions to my students' work, I rarely found it helpful. How *you* did it and how *I* did it, and how he or she will do it, were too inevitably different. I don't to my knowledge even share genes with anyone in this room, nor many other things that would influence our respective views of the world, so how might I be expected to tell anyone here how to compose his or her own testimony in verse?

Not that I won't touch at some length today on how I do it myself; it's only that I will do so in the modest hope that sharing my process may stir something in your own minds. Should that be so, you'll have to use whatever it is in your own way. I scarcely imagine you'll drop everything to follow me down my enlightened path,

The path isn't all that enlightened, actually. Indeed, I feel *awkward* as a writer most of the time, just as I often feel awkward as a man, as for example in speaking to you now. In fact, for me poetry, more than other genres I've practiced, is a crucial instrument for working with that very awkwardness. I've often claimed that that's a fair part of what poetry's *for*. If writing poems affords me a way of grappling with my awkwardness, in the process abating it some, I won't really care much about reputation, prizes, and other trappings of a so-called successful career. That may sound disingenuous, but it's true.

Back now briefly to the autobiographical trail I was trotting a few moments ago.

I came to a sustained writing habit very late, north of thirty-five when I started applying myself with real dedication, forty when my first collection appeared. Why should all that have been? Why hadn't I gone to a writing program like this one?

Truth is, even if I'd had enough on hand to present a portfolio (as I didn't), I wouldn't have found a tenth as many such programs in the middle '60s as now, a fact I mention neutrally, by the way. And even if

I'd thought of being a writer back in my twenties, I'd never have dreamed of applying to any of the few available institutions—to Iowa, say, or Stanford.

You see, I had this peculiar idea that writers knew some secret, and that they weren't about to share it with me. The ones who had that secret were the one or two I knew who did go on to MFA programs. (These students stopped writing almost immediately after finishing their degrees, by the way; make what you want of that.) Without access to their cabalistic knowledge, I'd soon be headed either to Viet Nam or to graduate school. Unlike my beloved roommate Phinney, who fell in that war, I chose the latter.

After my graduate years, and after twice as much time teaching conventional literature courses, indeed well after the average laboratory rat would have come upon it, I finally understood what the secret was: if you want to be a writer, you have to, like, *write.*

In my defense, my training as a scholar may have blinded me to this self-evident datum. Strange to say, most of my teachers, brilliant as a few of them were, had a strikingly adolescent view of what makes a poet. They believed that he or she just walks out one day, gets struck by lightning or the finger of God or whatever—and PRESTO: it's William Blake!

Small wonder I knew flat nothing about what being a writer involved. I had a pretty fancy PhD, and in pursuit of it had read a whole lot of canonical poetry. Largely on my own, I'd encountered the contemporary stars; but although I could have spun a pretty spiffy *interpretation* of poems by Lowell, Berryman, or Plath, that intellectual gambit would of course have helped me not at all in starting my own writing. I hadn't discovered, to put matters tersely, how I might read poetry as a poet. I couldn't yet read it, so to speak, from within. I still don't know which was chicken and which egg. Did I learn to read as a writer by writing, or did I learn to write by learning to read in a new way? It scarcely matters here.

I'll be speaking only of my own tendencies from this point on. As I've already implied, there are poets I love, even idolize, who do things far differently than I do. And of course there always have been. I think for instance of Alexander Pope, who writes what he specifically calls essays in verse: the *Essay on Man,* the *Essay on Criticism,* and so on. But I'm not about to be the Pope of poetry, or of anything else. My rational, formal-essayistic brain, a somewhat neglected organ anyhow, won't prevail in my take on the art.

For me, anyhow, poetry has become another way of *knowing,* in which black can be black but can also be white, though that is probably an overstatement and is surely a poetical figure. In any case, how does lyric lead on to knowledge, imperfect as the knowledge may prove? Time for a touch of that confessional mode: as I set out to discover what there is for me to know, I must first become, in Wallace Stevens's phrase, "an ignorant man again." I must proceed in such ignorance until the poem reveals the knowledge I've alluded to.

For fear that all this sound too dreadfully solipsistic, however, let me say that dealings with other people are as likely to spur me as any precious little *frisson* of private emotion. I must interact with family members, friends, community members, and people who never consider poetry at all, in my case, the likes of loggers and farmers. I think we poets need to have commerce with such folk, or their urban counterparts, lest we believe that everyone shares our fascinations, and lest we therefore write work based on such mistaken belief. If there's any danger at all in Creeping MFAism, it may be that we too often preach to our choir. Yet that's a different subject too, and I should be moving on in a more linear, focused way.

I'm afraid, however, that that's just not in me: I won't, I can't move straight ahead. Having, explicitly elsewhere and tacitly here, commended non-dialectical process to prospective poets, I will ask you to bear with me now as I make an apparently oblique leap. I want for a moment to remember a certain question recently asked of me in connection with an anthology scheme: "How has music influenced your writing?" I've offered my response in another place, and rather than repeating it here, I'll instead recite a draft poem of my own, also recent.

The one I have in mind began as I listened to a CD called *Know What I Mean?* featuring Cannonball Adderley (I've been on an Adderley jag since the '60s, Cannonball *and* his brother Nat). After just a few bars I suddenly thought back to the first time of many that I heard Cannonball's band in live performance. That was at a Philadelphia club called Pep's Musical Bar, which in those days was owned by basketball legend Wilt Chamberlain. It must have been in February of 1965, because just at that moment Dr. King and his followers were being brutalized in Selma, Alabama. I had worked as a tutor in the north end of Philadelphia the summer before, and was back for a visit.

As I tried many years later to recall that particular time in my life and the nation's, in due course I came up with the following:

MERCY, MERCY, MERCY

The Stilt, some called him. Or the Big Dipper.
Chamberlain was the man, for whom
they changed the rules, because one night

41

he scored 100 points in a game.
And Wilt was the owner of Pep's Café.
Broad and South, Philadelphia,
1965, where the great
Cannonball Adderley band of the time,
with Cannon himself on alto, his brother
Nat on cornet, Joe Zawinul
on keyboard, Yusef Lateef on tenor,
Sam Jones on bass and Louis Hayes, drums—
that Adderley band was turning out

the whole damned place, it was standing room only,
and there I was standing in a jam-packed aisle
between bar and booths, in love with sound.
How precise it is, the way I remember
that Yusef had launched into *Gemini*
when I felt the tap on my shoulder and turned
and looked straight into the middle button
of a splash-weave jacket and heard a voice say
from way up there, *Pardon me, white man.*
What else on earth would I do but pardon?
I felt that *I* was the one who needed
pardon, not because I felt fear,
as I might have, the man being more than tall,

the man being wide as a truck as well,
which you couldn't tell on television—
it wasn't fear, but rather the utter
incapacity, my own
or anyone else's, to take that night
and the muted light and the mellow liquor
feeling and to blow every bit of all that
out into air in one big breath,
so the breath would somehow change the world
that I knew surrounded everybody.
Dr. King was trying to change it
in spite of frothing dogs and cops.
You watched it every day on t.v.

The clubs. The cattle prods. Perhaps,
though I was just 22, this was
my first real understanding of how
goodwill *can* count for nothing and magic
thinking will buy you at best another
beer if you can make your way

> —*pardon me, pardon me, pardon me, pardon me*—
> past those suave black bodies and up to the bar
> and make yourself heard over harmonies
> and tumbles down into dissonance
> and back of the white-hot reeds and brass,
> above the drums, above the pulsing
> wrenching chords that Joe broke into
>
> next on *Mercy, Mercy, Mercy.*

What are the ingredients that went into this poem's "knowledge," as in my vanity I name it? First off, and of course unknown to the reader, I'd been listening to that CD, though the sidemen there are different from the ones I refer to in the poem. There was surely other hidden stuff too, which no reader could possibly know. *Every* poem, I believe, has its hidden allegory in addition to its overt material, so that none is ever entirely understandable, even to its author.

But I also believe that every poem has its own somewhat esoteric *formal* impulses too. Let's look at those first. I discovered that my rushed, more or less free-verse first draft ended up with fifty-four lines. That allowed me to try dividing it into six stanzas of nine lines; then nine stanzas of six lines. When neither worked for me, I cut one line from the whole and generated four stanzas of thirteen lines with a final one-line stanza that came down hard on the title of the tune.

Now resorting to mere addition, subtraction, and division probably sounds mechanical as can be, and in some sense doubtless is; yet for me it's also liberating, because such measures distract me from over-managing my assumed thematics. The fiddling with line-count sets me loose to play with my materials, which for a poet are words and lines and stanzas, just as for the musician they're notes, phrases, chord structures, scales.

As I reflected on the six-line stanza, on the nine-, and ultimately on the thirteen-, my effort (and in two of the three tries my failure) to make each one not only a component of the whole but also a more or less self-contained unit allowed certain thematic possibilities to sneak up on me. I did not have to will them into existence. If meaning, to call it that, did enter, it did so unbidden. By letting associations forge themselves, not foisting them into its fabric, I released my poem, as I put the notion earlier, to be what *it* wanted to be.

As I also said earlier, my goal as a teacher is to help my students do the same, which means they must learn to pick up on the clues that their own words and forms inevitably plant in beginning drafts. Here, the title of the tune I used as the last line, "Mercy, Mercy, Mercy," simply leapt to mind when I was looking for closure; it is, I think, the one component of the poem that never changed. "Mercy, Mercy, Mercy" was not, I believe, the tune that played just after Wilt tapped me on the shoulder, but it certainly should have been, as the other parts of the poem suddenly made clear. If the poem's concerns came unbidden, they came a bit discomfitingly too. *Mercy* seemed to have something to do with the word *pardon* in Chamberlain's "Pardon me," though the politeness of his request was more than a little sarcastic.

Now before I began, my will may have wanted this poem to evoke transport by music, but it seems the poem itself was looking for something else: when the tune's title dropped down in so crucial a place in the draft, I came to recognize the part of guilt in what I'd thought to be my goodwill that evening. There was something about *me* that begged pardon. Maybe deep down, far as I may have been from some frothing white supremacist, I understood myself as at least tangentially implicated in that disgrace at Selma. I was, after all, an American of primarily European stock.

And finally, straightforward as it may appear, "Mercy, Mercy, Mercy" being a 4/4 tune, I decided to write my poem in tetrameter, another choice that pulled me away from worrying too greatly about so-called theme. I wanted more to enact the evening, you see, than overtly to comment on it.

That moment in Pep's; that eye-blink encounter with Big Wilt; that rendition of "Mercy, Mercy, Mercy," a tune I hadn't yet heard from the Adderley band—all of this got tied up in memory with the violence confronted by that era's civil rights activists all over the country. It's more than possible it got tied up as well with the fact that Joe Zawinul, the featured musician and the author of the song, was the only white musician in the quintet. He'd found entrée to a world that I revered, but one that—however much I tried to tell myself otherwise—remained pretty opaque to a young Ivy Leaguer like me. To recall my words from earlier on, the profound sense of my own awkwardness, then and much later, leaped back into consciousness.

It may on first inspection appear strange for me now to say that everything I've discussed has something to do with poetry as *play*. Think, however, of the several meanings of that term: it may be play in the sense of drama; but perhaps it's play too in the sense of playing around with one's materials, like children in a sandbox, and no shame in that; finally, it may be play in more or less the same sense we use the term when we speak of a musician's performance.

Where can all this play take us? Well, maybe it can lift us out of our very awkwardness, or at least into a more clear-eyed contemplation of it. And this is the heart of the excitement—I can't call it less—that our art has always stirred in my being, as I hope it does in yours.

NOTE

   1. Addressed to students in the MFA Program at the University of North Carolina, Wilmington, May 2007.

Making a Case; or,
"Where Are You Coming From?"

⸺⧽⧼⸺

IN THE LATE '70s, I read an essay by Brendan Galvin on poems he
called "Mumblings," in which an unidentified *I* "tries to tell the reader
how he ought to feel about the nonspecific predicament of another, often unspecified person."[1] Yes, I thought, or else the poet addresses an
unidentified second person about the cloudy difficulties of his or her
relationship with that second person, or yet a third, also unidentified. I,
too, disliked the verse Galvin attacked, especially for its evident assumption that A Poet, merely by so designating him- or herself, could
lay claim to an interesting inner life. Surely, I believed, an "I" was interesting only if he or she proved to be, which meant among other things
that she or he must cogently reveal an identity in the writing itself.

My recourse was rash. I founded a magazine. Its poetry, I vowed,
would seek more accessible premises. "Pronouns are not people": I yet
recall that cautionary dictum on certain early rejection notes, one that
unquestionably smacked of the tyro's glibness. But I still approve its
gist.

Not that all '70s poets mumbled in the way Brendan had mocked.
Some relied on image, whether deep or shallow, plain or surreal. And
yet these writers, too, seemed often to exclude me from their work's
deeper resonances. Just as I was expecting some authorial commitment,
a poet would turn to notice, say, a pigeon carrying a snip of someone's
necktie through a raincloud, or whatever. Subject matter, so to speak,
never quite came out in public.

Somebody once accused Edmund Wilson of identifying all things
he couldn't do as vices while elevating his aptitudes into virtues. I want
not to do the same: if for example I've always inclined, almost compul-
sively, to narrative, I've never dogmatically urged the same bent on anyone else, in part because I mustn't deprive myself of a Donald Justice,
whose approach I'll never emulate, no matter how deeply I admire it.
Nor, among more junior poets, would I avoid Charles Simic, William
Matthews, Marilyn Hacker, merely to cite a few most divergent cases.

Twelve years ago, though, nettled by the self-regard in certain '70s
verse, I did couch my editorial commentary in narrative terms, initiat-
ing, moreover, an annual *New England Review* narrative poetry competi-

tion. And by 1982, many of my own readings included "The Feud," a fifteen-page verse tale from my second collection. The rancor I felt against excessive personalism found a momentary release in story, or perhaps more properly in character, a concern I sensed we might too easily have ceded to the prose writers.

My pitch, however fresh in those years, is commonplace now, when many commentators—not all of them clearheaded or well informed— assert that hyper-privacy has lost our poetry a readership, and this despite the fact that verse today is generally less "difficult"—think of Andrew Hudgins or C. K. Williams—than it was a decade ago. There's also a movement abroad called the New Narrative.

I've recently wondered why, having once stumped so for narrative, I want now, both as writer and critic, to move on. It isn't only that I'd avoid committing that Wilsonian error, in the manner, sometimes, of the more doctrinaire exponents of the New Narrative; more importantly, my *tendency* to narrative was always of greater moment to me than story-line itself. If narrative served to brake my own narcissism, as pronounced as anyone's, it also provided a more positive, and more intriguing impulse: it opened my poems to rhetoric, by which I, like Jonathan Holden,[2] mean the language of persuasion, argument, testimony, even of the very abstraction that Ezra the Ur-Imagist warned us to go in fear of. (I speak here of immediately recognizable stuff, not of the rhetorical *gestures* that I think all good poems contain.)

But why was rhetoric, so understood, a goal at all? Having not only lectured but also visited many a workshop, I had noticed, in addition to and continuous with "mumbling," a kind of anti-rhetorical rhetoric among participants: "Show, Don't Tell." Over and over I heard it; and at length I bridled, thankful that most canonical poets had never heeded such an injunction. Consider:

> The ceremony of innocence is drowned;
> The best lack all conviction, while the worst
> Are full of passionate intensity.

Even though Yeats himself polarized rhetoric (made of our quarrels with others) and poetry (made of quarrels with ourselves), he went ahead and composed that great sector of "The Second Coming."

Or, for further example:

> Getting and spending we lay waste our powers.
> Little we see in Nature that is ours . . . ;

Time present and time past
are both perhaps included in time future . . . ;

I have wasted my life . . .

Publication—is the Auction
Of the mind of Man—
Poverty—be justifying
For so foul a Thing . . .

I saw the best minds of my generation . . . etc.

The list could be endlessly extended, but whatever our tastes, few would think immediately to send Tom, Jim, Emily, William, and Allen back to workshop for the sin of too much telling. And would any of us really scold John, on the same grounds, for the following lines, of which I'll presently make a good deal?

"Beauty is truth, truth beauty,"—that is all
Ye know on earth, and all ye need to know.

I spent much breath on the virtues of narrative in my early years as editor, teacher, and lecturer; but privately I wanted sanction in my own writing for moves like those above. Indeed, I've composed relatively few pure narrative poems in my five collections to date, a fact that surprises me less today than once it might have, since I see that from early on I sought not so much the freedom to make a story as to make a case—perhaps like Frost's in "Two Tramps in Mudtime," to choose one more instance:

My object in living is to unite
My avocation and my vocation
As my two eyes make one in sight.
Only where love and need are one,
And the work is play for mortal stakes,
Is the deed ever really done
For Heaven and the future's sakes.

It was not restraint alone, then, that barred me from cajoling fellow poets into narrative-or-nothing, that made me hedge my bets, proposing storyteller's *values* instead. Yes, I believed, if I could establish characters, including the character called "I"; if I could suggest setting, historical, political, geographical; if I could at least imply plot; if in short I could call back to our service some basics of conventional fiction, the reader might accept my trucking with big issues, like the perils of revenge in "The Feud."

The real goal, however, was to find modes of argument in verse. And if I still feel that narrative can help a poet make a case, I'm increasingly interested in how she or he may do so otherwise, in how authors gain author-ity for overt rhetoric, for assertion, information, and so on, without recourse to fiction's tools. How can Keats write that "Beauty is truth" and impel us to deep thought, whereas, whimsically to choose a '70s instance, the originator of "Happiness Is a Warm Puppy" impels me to fantasies of violence, even though that aphorism and Keats's exactly share rhetorical structure.

I ask you now to remember, precisely, "Ode on a Grecian Urn." The poem, of course, will remain inexhaustible, and my quirky responses will scarcely put its complexities to rest. For one thing, poems can have equal and opposite pulls, as Keats knew better than most. And I'm reacting here not as critic but as writer; there's nothing scholarly, then, in my observing that

—Keats calls the scene on the urn a love scene, but it's actually one of intended *rape*, the maidens being understandably "loath," "struggl[ing] to escape," a fact that alone must give us pause if we want to discover the oft-alleged "calm" of the work;
—the urn is said "to express a flowery tale more sweetly than our rhyme": if so, to put it crudely, we poets must despair;
—all the questions in the opening strophe concern the referentiality of the urn's images: where's the scene? what's the legend? who are the figures? Keats can't even tell if these are last human or divine. In short, the questions are about plot, setting, and character;
—they're rhetorical questions, the answer to each being "I don't know."

Let's start with that last point. Keats asks his questions in response to the urn's images—which "show." The poet will later make clear, prosodically stressing the word itself, that image cannot "tell." I think this has consequences, say, for the famous opening of part 2:

> Heard melodies are sweet, but those unheard
> Are sweeter; therefore, ye soft pipes, play on;
> Not to the sensual ear, but, more endeared,
> Pipe to the spirit ditties of no tone. . . .

The cheerful reading is that Keats's "negative capability" imagines his writing a poem even as he recognizes its inferiority to a certain silence: that of pure image, of scenery transcending "All breathing human passion." I won't merely appeal to the fact that this desire for a stasis removed from passional life, and from the need to testify until the tongue goes dry, simply seems un-Keatsian. Consider instead where the second stanza's assertions point: to the turn in stanza 4, with its emphasis on "sacrifice." The "melodist" of the prior strophe, "happy" in his quiet, and the "more happy love! more happy, happy love!" (does Keats protest too much?) have both vanished, not to return.

Keats, in brief, now recognizes the poverty of his prior claims, that silence and slow time are superior to human emotion, unheard airs to heard, unknowable characters, settings, and legends to knowable. Such contentions lead to a dead end, at least for a poet. If Keats reverts to his rhetorical questions in this fourth and pivotal stanza, the answer to each is still "I don't know," which means, among other things, "I can make no case." No longer affirming such ignorance and powerlessness, nor finding mere image "more endeared" than testimony, the author concedes that

> . . . little town, thy streets forevermore
> Will silent be; and not a soul to tell
> Why thou art desolate, can e'er return.

I'd once have claimed that the poet here craves a narrative solution, is "desolate" himself because there's "not a soul to tell"—even on the simplest level—what the urn's depictions enact or signify. Be that as it may, Keats has by the end established a dialectic: silence/speech; image/articulation; showing/telling:

> O Attic shape! Fair attitude! with brede
> Of marble men and maidens overwrought,
> With forest branches and the trodden weed;
> Thou, silent form, dost tease us out of thought
> As doth eternity: Cold Pastoral!
> When old age shall this generation waste,
> Thou shalt remain, in midst of other woe
> Than ours, a friend to man, to whom thou say'st
> "Beauty is truth, truth beauty,"—that is all
> Ye know on earth, and all ye need to know.

That final aphorism is often taken as a further sign of Keats's negative capability: he persists in responding to beauty, even though verbal beauty is *ignis fatuus* compared to that of wrought things. Indeed, some claim that the very stateliness of the ode—its grand rhythms and intricate structure—paradoxically proves this "heard melody" to be as dignified and enduring as the urn's "silent form," which has teased the poet out of thought, collapsing the dialectical values I've just mentioned. In this manner, the abstraction "Beauty" destroys the proclivity Keats ascribed to Coleridge, "an irritable reaching after fact and reason," in the very letter that coined the term *negative capability*.

This reading seems sentimental to me, for if the silent urn teases Keats out of thought, it does so "as doth eternity." This is not, however, to identify poem and urn *sub specie aeternitatis,* but to see eternity as a succubus, reminding Keats, quite understandably, of mortality. To think of the urn is to think of a burial vessel or a grave. Hence, famously, the *Cold* Pastoral that the poet evokes:

> When old age shall this generation waste,
>> Thou shalt remain, *in midst of other woe.* . . .

The phrase I've emphasized is, I think, artfully enjambed, the break allowing us to imagine, at least momentarily, that the urn is itself a woe as durable as others. Further, the silent image—"marble men and maidens overwrought"—is associated with wasted "generation," and thus, etymologically, with the ruin both of genius and of procreation, including its "breathing human passion." If the urn, in and of itself, is man's friend, then man as poet needs no enemies.

The brilliant Dartmouth professor James Cox once joked to me that Keats must perform an unspeakable act on the "unravished bride of quietness" in order for her finally to speak. It was, of course, a joke, and outrageous, but only because the closing pronouncement is surely not speechless urn's but poet's. And, as nonspecific and abstract as it is, how can it be other than tepid self-consolation? Even if I could somehow imagine it as the urn's utterance, I'd be reminded of a bad parent's response to the child who thirsts for explanation: "Why can't I go outside?" "Because I said so; *that's all you need to know.*"

"'Beauty is truth, truth beauty'—that is all": the line is also linked by rhyme to "Cold Pastoral!" And, reading on, we find it's "all ye know *on earth.*" Is there some different venue, then? Yes, but a lesser poem of May 1819, the "Ode on Melancholy," warns against it:

> No, no, go not to Lethe, neither twist
> Wolfsbane, tight-rooted, for its poisonous wine;
> Nor suffer thy pale forehead to be kissed

By nightshade, ruby grape of Proserpine;
Make not your rosary of yew-berries,
Nor let the beetle, nor the death-moth be
Your mournful Psyche, nor the downy owl
A partner in your sorrow's mysteries;
For shade to shade will come too drowsily,
And drown the wakeful anguish of the soul.

It's wrong, as Keats puts it in the more famous nightingale ode, even to be "half in love with easeful death." True, he says,

Now more than ever seems it rich to die,
To cease upon the midnight with no pain,
While thou art pouring forth thy soul abroad
In such an ecstacy! . . .

But here's the conclusion of that stanza:

Still wouldst thou sing, and I have ears in vain—
To thy high requiem become a sod.

Just as, without a mediating authorial presence, the visual image of an urn is cold, without that presence the song of a nightingale is so much mere sound. Imagination, figured as Psyche in yet another ode, demands votive testimony. Otherwise, she's bereft, having

No voice, no lute, no incense sweet
From chain-swung censer teeming;
No shrine, no grove, no oracle, no heat
Of pale-mouthed prophet dreaming. . . .

A central issue in all these spring odes, I believe, is the poet's need, precisely, to tell. In the nightingale poem, Keats dreams of fading far away, forgetting "the weariness, the fever, and the fret, / Here, where men sit and hear each other groan." He will fly to his ease on the "viewless wings of Poesy," again removing himself somehow from passionate speech. But where does that leave him? "I cannot see what flowers are at my feet, / Nor what soft incense hangs upon the boughs, / But in embalmèd darkness, guess each sweet. . . ." There is that hint of the grave, once more, in the play on "embalmed."

If, in "Ode on a Grecian Urn," plain image is married to muteness, in "Ode to a Nightingale" we see how feckless, perhaps even deadly, is visionary image. Indeed visionary image (we might say "deep image" today) is oxymoronic for Keats; it is "viewless"—i.e., invisible—and therefore guesswork. It reduces him to passivity ("Darkling, I listen"), and, worst, it's a fraud. The poet at last acknowledges that his ode, conventional invocation of a spiritual presence, has here only invoked brief illusion:

> Adieu! the fancy cannot cheat so well
> As she is famed to do, deceiving elf.

If "Ode to a Nightingale" poses different rhetorical questions from those of the urn poem, still their answer is, categorically, "I don't know."

> Was it a vision, or a waking dream?
> Fled is that music—Do I wake or sleep?

My excerpts are of course selective, but they dramatize a dilemma of poetry now as then: we must attend to what Richard Wilbur has more lately called "the things of this world"; and yet we cannot be content with them, no matter how splendidly or grimly graphic they may be. The music flees if we rely on simple image, as Keats first tries to do in contemplating his urn; but if we dissociate ourselves from simple image and seek some visionary realm, such music as we get is ersatz or worse. We need, as always, a poetry incorporating both image and something non-visionary beyond it—something that may, yes, involve narrative values but may, by my argument, involve rhetorical ones in addition. Or instead.

I'm campaigning for overt rhetoric, which will not be to the taste of all. And yet one way or another, poetry will make a case, else it will cease to function as verbal art, earning its praise in other terms—making "a good picture," say, or having "good music." In which instances, why substitute verse for an accomplished painting? Or as Marvin Bell has cogently asked, "If a poem is only music, what chance does it have against real music?"

In what I consider his greatest composition, Keats exemplifies an attitude not yet discovered in the great spring odes I've touched on. Originally composed in September of the miraculous year, "To Autumn" shows a familiar ploy of rhetorical questioning: "Where are the songs of Spring?"—which must certainly include the odes to which I've alluded from the May preceding—"Aye, where are they?" (stanza 3). The answer, however wistful, goes somewhat beyond the familiar "I don't know":

Think not of them, thou hast thy music too. . . .

This Septembral music, to be sure, is also prepared to "flee." The choir of gnats, the bleat of lambs no longer lambs, the songs of fall insects and migratory birds constitute a collective *memento mori*, yet the poem itself is mellow and fruitful. One could read the whole renowned last stanza as a gentle Imagist piece, the more imagistic and gentle as it moves to closure. We may think of Stevens's famous claim that "Death is the mother of beauty." And yet where is a similar rhetoric here?

Well, let me say for now that there are many ways to skin the rhetorical cat, and let me momentarily swerve from "To Autumn"'s strategies in order to consider one of those ways. I look ahead to Robert Frost, and to a poem whose rhetoric is easy to hear, since that's about all there is: "Provide, Provide" is chiefly persuasion, verging even on preachiness. It offers four short lines of showing—

> The witch that came (the withered hag)
> To wash the steps with pail and rag,
> Was once the beauty Abishag,
>
> The picture pride of Hollywood.—

and seventeen of telling.

The lines that "show" are narrative, however minimal (and however short, incidentally, on image): Famous beauty becomes crone. On the strength of this short-short story, the author moves straight to rhetoric, which begins as wry musing (lines 5–15) and, though Frost doesn't purge the wryness (he rarely does, in any poem), concludes as realist argument:

> No memory of having starred
> Atones for later disregard,
> Or keeps the end from being hard.
>
> Better to go down dignified
> With boughten friendship at your side
> Than none at all. Provide, provide!

If you agree that Frost here "gets away with" flouting the show-don't-tell mantra, you may say that he does so exactly because, in that opening mini-narrative, he *has* shown, and I won't disagree. My point, however, will be that narrativity is only one of the many ways, to repeat my inelegant figure, of skinning that cat of rhetoric. If character, setting, and plot—narrative components—validate the author's point of view in "Provide, Provide," I want to consider other modes of validation. For, however achieved, authorial and authoritative point of view is what's ultimately of consequence here: his or her authority will be the energy persuading us to hear out whatever case a poet may make.

Even though, for example, I took the pronouncement ironically, I heard Keats out when he said that beauty was truth. No, I didn't believe him, or even believe he believed himself. But the very dialectical structure of the poem, with its attendant tonal changes, told me enough of the speaker that I could share in his ponderings. I witnessed how the urn's depictions provoked the loaded questions in "Ode on a Grecian Urn," but also saw that these mere images could not respond to those unsettling questions. As Stanley Plumly has said, "The image has no voice." It was Keats's own voice I heard: confronted with silence, it articulated an attitude—not "fair" like the urn's but troubled, complex—within the poem. In brief, it summoned me to participate in the author's quarrel with himself, which, for all of Yeats, resulted in rhetoric . . . and in poetry also. In rhetorical poetry.

We do not participate; we reject or scoff or get angry when we read "Happiness Is a Warm Puppy," because it suggests no specifiable attitude, is enounced by no identifiable voice, signals no well-grounded point of view. Where, to gloss the old '60s phrase of my subtitle, is such a proposition coming from? That's another rhetorical question, the self-evident answer being our old, dismaying "I don't know." The puppy-slogan is argument, yes, but free-floating argument. It rides off into the distance as if on an automobile bumper, leaving me, at least, to thunder: WHO SAYS SO?

Whatever it may do on a bumper sticker, in any case, argument or rhetoric in poems must not hover in such middle air. Indeed, by my interpretation of the "Grecian Urn," it was just such hovering that Keats found insufficient, even deathly. Knowing the gesture to be somehow both aesthetically and philosophically wrong, still he wrote, "Beauty is truth, truth beauty," consciously *allowing* the aphorism to waft upward from its own silent, imagistic context and thus to reveal its desperate breathiness, irrelevance. Only a very great poet, of course, would choose so daring a gambit, would trot out the very mistake he implicitly warns against, would permit his rhetoric to "float free" by way of indicating the perils of such a technique.

"To Autumn" moves me particularly in that Keats, by now deathly ill, not only accepts but also affirms the dislocation of his ego, his "I," from the center of his meditation, seeking to fuse it with a greater general process. In the ode on the urn, as I've just suggested, the quest for authority had led to an all but crippling doubt. Indeed, in *all* the songs of spring Keats's would-be prophet's voice clamored for a spirit's ear, and always unsuccessfully. Now he does not even try to invoke the goddess, doesn't have to: she's already there in quotidian reality. Far from claiming some "Romantic" special province for The Poet, then, some insight that only his point of view can muster, the author figures himself as just another observer.

The poem is, paradoxically, great in its posture of modesty. Just so, its rhetoric is compelling in its hiddenness. For if "To Autumn" does possess rhetoric, it seems strangely unconnected with argument. There's no equivalent of "Beauty is truth." Poetic argument instead relies for its effect on the institution of perspective, which, ironically, the poem then seeks to dismantle. This is the greatest paradox of all here: that by first vigorously establishing it, the author persuades us to surrender personal point of view as a vanity. Indeed, the desirability of such surrender is the very object of his rhetoric; but it's achieved by exquisitely subtle devices.

Thus the opening stanza heaps up its imagery, from which the rhetoric—indirect, quiet—takes its resonance. The world is initially shown to be so abundant that the bees "*think* warm days will never cease. . . ." But the irrelevance of even such comparatively innocent ego is made clear by the lines that open the second section of the ode:

> Who hath not seen thee oft amid thy store?
> Sometimes whoever seeks abroad may find
> Thee sitting careless on a granary floor. . . .

That is: I, the poet, have seen the goddess amid all her sweet trappings, but then, who hasn't? Even the birds and beasts are witnesses. The author immediately reverts to images, which now collude with the rhetoric, just as the rhetoric has colluded with the imagery. But the central point is that neither is sufficient of itself. Let me further attempt to clarify this tricky contention by rehearsal of that "Imagist poem" in stanza 3:

> Where are the songs of Spring? Aye, where are they?
> Think not of them, thou hast thy music too—
> While barrèd clouds bloom the soft-dying day,
> And touch the stubble-plains with rosy hue;
> Then in a wailful choir the small gnats mourn
> Among the river sallows, borne aloft
> Or sinking as the light wind lives or dies;
> And full-grown lambs loud bleat from hilly bourn;

Hedge crickets sing; and now with treble soft
The redbreast whistles from a garden-croft;
And gathering swallows twitter in the skies.

The same rhythms prevail: the passage begins in rhetoric, in "loaded" questions, so that the return to imagery—the purest in the poem—remains grounded in the quietly argumentative attitude: the very unloading of the language as the stanza progresses suggests the case being made. We have wailful gnats that *mourn;* we have "full-grown lambs," sheep ready for slaughter, so that there's some poignance in their *bleat.* But the crickets merely *sing,* the swallows *twitter.*

Keats has moved from images of sight to the cruder ones of hearing; but more importantly, his very verbs of sound grow increasingly generic, almost hackneyed, surely vernacular. His choice of words implies, again, that he is no longer *the* testifier but *a* testifier, common as the animals. Indeed he wants to extinguish his Self's view by conjoining it with a kind of general perspective.

However, in lyric, which for this reason distinguishes itself from certain fictional possibilities, by the way, there can *be* no general perspective. Lyrical point of view is never omniscient, is always limited; and what I'm addressing, finally, is how the limits get established within a given poem. When I say rhetoric must have authority; when I say I want to know where such and such a rhetorical gesture is coming from, be it overt (e.g., "The best lack all conviction") or more latent (e.g., that progressive subversion of image's significance in "To Autumn"); when I say I want to know on what grounds a poem's case is being made—it's point of view that actually concerns me.

Whenever we lyricists engage in acts of argument, as I hope we will, or even of gentle persuasion, it's a good idea to ask those same slightly wisecrack questions of ourselves, or rather of our poems, that we might ask of the bumper-sticker slogan: *Who says so? Where are you coming from?* If we can't answer on the basis of what we have written, we have let our pronouncements float free, and they too will be no more than slogans, irksome in their assumption of authority. Authoritative point of view must be earned, as the Puritans say. Nor am I saying anything much different: to make our cases in poetic format, we must establish our credentials; that is the crucial end, though the means to it are likely infinite.

In any event, I suspect that every access to authoritative point of view will lead, as each has with Keats, into considerations of voice. And yet voice can be established, too, in countless ways: by the things or images a poem talks about ("To Autumn"); by its grammar and syntax (those of Marianne Moore in "Poetry" are exemplary in this respect); by exploitation of structure ("Ode on a Grecian Urn" could be studied from this angle as well as all the others), including responses, obedient or rebellious, to received formal structures (like the sonnet, with its promise of high seriousness, the villanelle, which implies obsession, or the couplet, with its yen for aphorism), and so on. But vocal authority, however accomplished, is essential. If, having composed a draft of a lyric, we ask ourselves *Who says so?*, we must have a more compelling answer than naked "I."

NOTES

This essay was originally delivered as a lecture at The Robert Frost Place, Franconia, New Hampshire, in August 1989.

1. Brendan Galvin, "The Mumbling of Young Werther: Angst by Blueprint in Contemporary Poetry," *Ploughshares* 4, no. 3 (1978): 122.

2. See Jonathan Holden, *The Rhetoric of the Contemporary Lyric* (Bloomington: Indiana University Press, 1980). Readers will also recognize a kind of general debt to Robert Pinsky's seminal *The Situation of Poetry*.

The Knife, a Parable

A FEW YEARS PAST, my family spent a summer in Italy. I was teaching poetry in a so-called workshop, which was peopled almost exclusively by Americans of middle age, the majority women. They were a likeable group, though few in fact were primarily interested in becoming or growing as poets. Perhaps this should have troubled me more than it did: they were there largely because they wanted a Tuscan sojourn, but after all, my family wanted the same.

I eased my compunctions by thinking I could say something to each participant about the workings of imagination as it applied to the composition of poems. This would at worst make them more attentive readers, if readers they would be. I admit that I left my rationale at that, for fear reflection might reveal it to be capricious and shallow.

Ours was a little town south of Siena, where we befriended a number of native citizens, especially one local family. Our fourteen-year-old son became particularly fond of the family's only child, a boy named Ugo, also fourteen. Though we had tried as best we could to teach our own son some Italian, he had virtually none: nevertheless, he and Ugo—who knew only a few more words of English than his new pal did of Italian—spent hours in one another's company, conversing in a kind of lingua franca, along with physical gesture.

Those two laughed a lot, above all at one another's pantomimes, each deliberately making up a far different story from what the other intended. This led to silly, indelible adventures, all innocent enough.

One Wednesday, the two went to the open market in the city, and Ugo bought a knife there. It was a tacky item, not made in Italy but probably in some Third World sweatshop, so that when he brought it home, his mother scolded him for throwing his cash at such junk. But Ugo had been caught by the look of its plastic handles, colored, unconvincingly, like rosewood, and the shiny ersatz-chrome button that released the dull, finger-sized blade. He noticed how the blade threw back the sun pouring over the east wall of Siena. Or so our son told us, on the basis of his companion's small utterances and bodily movements.

All these things must have conspired in making the knife Ugo's heart's desire. Images, many from the American action-hero comics that he devoured, may have crowded his mind. But what could he really do with the knife? He likely had no idea. I suspect he just wanted to *own* it, to make it part of some tale that he hadn't even composed as yet.

Shortly afterward, he lost the knife while he and our son were playing soccer with some other local teenagers in Buonconvento, Ugo's town, as it had been the town of his family for generations. He cursed, the aspirated *t*'s of his region, a remnant from ancient Moorish times there, roughening the liquid Latin of his speech and amusing our son, who reported the scene that evening at supper. Like his brother and sisters, he has always been a very good mimic, and we all laughed at his little performance. We could almost see and hear Ugo himself.

From that moment, I have nothing to go on but imagination. We are home in Vermont now, with its intense October foliage, not the summery lemon and beige of the Tuscan landscape, the muted pinks and ivories of its architecture.

Ugo and our son exchanged letters for a few months, though their need to find translators became cumbersome, and silence arrived soon enough; my wife and I likewise exchanged a few postcards with Ugo's parents, but these too stopped within a year.

Of course we all have memories of our stay, some of them pretty odd. The youngest girl remembers a myna bird in a local restaurant, for example, which would now and then break from its busy whistling to cry *Santa Maria!* She still wonders why it was this short phrase that the bird had been taught, or had learned on its own. The girl was only seven during that visit, and shortly after our return to the United States, she made up a history in which the bird had escaped from a nasty priest, one who was mean to children. She related her narrative in a surprisingly lighthearted way, though, even the parts that involved the evil cleric's beatings of little boys and girls.

In my sixties now, I blend my own memories with the many others I retain not just from traveling to Buonconvento but to many other places too, before and after that summer—in fact all over the European and North American continents. My fatherhood figures in these recollections; so do a marriage and divorce, a blessed remarriage, a reasonably successful writing career, and certain bittersweet moments from when I was the age of my son and his Italian friend on the day they took a bus to the market.

Several nights ago, for instance, I dreamed of a girl named Patty, who threw me over for someone from another school. His name was Jimmy, a nice enough guy, but one whose very sight from that day forward made me embarrassed, lonely, sad, and furious all at once, because I thought I'd never live without Patty.

In the dream, she simply told me again what she told me then: *It's over.* Her face looked grim as death. I woke up in actual tears, and then I smiled at the uncanniness and downright absurdity of the mind let loose by sleep; and yet the dream had cut me, well, like a knife. This effect didn't have so much to do with the details I'd dreamed, which evaporated instantly, as with that very abstraction, *Loss.*

I never imagined I'd be able to say "I'm sixty." Now that I am, it can be easy to lapse into doldrums, so *much* losing itself as time lopes by: friends dropping of sudden heart seizures or vicious cancers, dogs' short spans running out, certain physical skills and mental faculties ebbing. Having responsibilities, however, not least to myself, I do whatever I can to avert or at least temper such moods when they come on. Besides, my life is everything a reasonable person might want. If I allowed only gloom to sink into me as I write this, I'd be a spoiled old fool.

And in my capacity as fool, I might imagine the knife come into some hoodlum's possession. There'd be a fight, a wounding, maybe even a mortal one. I could use Jimmy, or someone like him, either as perpetrator or victim, and, either way, purge my old resentment of him, though truth is I more or less forgot that resentment as soon as I went on to yet another adolescent love interest. She was Louise, pretty, my grandmother said, as a picture. I wonder where she may be.

In any case, I choose just now to think of another girl, whom I'll call Catiuccia. I have her pick up Ugo's little knife from the ground the boys have scuffed in their games in Buonconvento's tiny piazza. Having little interest in it, she stashes the knife in a paper box under her bed. She doesn't tell anyone about it, and maybe for its very secrecy she likes the fact that the knife lies there beneath her. There are nights when she can almost feel its presence, as if it had a heat or an electricity, as if it were something other than a cheap toy. She's only fourteen.

Two years go by and she meets a boy at the Festa di Sant' Anna, in which the town serves free sausages and pasta, a band plays, there is dancing (though she doesn't dance herself that day). There's also sentimental, clichéd speechifying by local dignitaries. Of course, she knows who the boy is, but has never spoken to him much beyond *Ciao.*

The girl has never before felt any attraction to boys, or none at least like what she now feels to Stefano. He is sixteen, not so much older than she, though the gap between sixteen and fourteen seems almost generational at that time of our lives, so that Stefano strikes her as a hopelessly remote prize. This depresses Catiuccia in a way she has never experienced either.

The girl tries to think of a way to impress Stefano, right there at the festival, mere feet from where she first found the knife—which she presents to him, hoping against all odds that he will somehow fall in love with her on the spot, despite their disparate ages, or at least will show some regard for her. But what Catiuccia senses, and admires, in Stefano is a certain quality of intellect, something almost bookish in his manner and in the few words they exchange. That quality, to her painful embarrassment, makes him no more interested in the knife than she really is.

Immediately feeling his lack of enthusiasm, she feels her poor heart buckle. Catiuccia runs home to castigate herself: a thing with a blade must be the exact opposite of anything Stefano stands for, or wants to stand for. She has recognized this far too late, and the very thought of her own clumsiness makes her chew her auburn hair and weep. She throws the empty little shoebox into a bin in the kitchen, and soaks her pillow for a night or two.

A few weeks later, on a stay with his Umbrian cousins, Stefano deliberately leaves his gift knife on a bench in Perugia, strangely reluctant just to drop it into some trash receptacle. Within the hour, another Tuscan boy, visiting relatives too, picks the knife from the bench. He's a boy named Ugo, one whom Catiuccia also knows, Buonconvento no more than a village after all.

Ugo is very pleased with his find. Maybe he even thanks the God he recently cursed for restoring the same sort of knife to him as the one he'd lost. He can't of course know that it's actually the very knife he bought in our son's company. But it's not so much the knife anyhow as the lucky fact of restitution that delights him so. It's as though he were blessed somehow.

A few days after coming home, standing in his room, the boy absent-mindedly pushes the bright button, shooting the blade out. He refolds the knife, pushes the button, refolds—and suddenly understands that he's bored, that he's playing with his knife for no other reason, that rather than relieving his ennui, in fact the knife deepens it. He throws his treasure out the open window, where it falls at the feet of Catiuccia, who makes a startled sound. Ugo rushes to the window, anxious. Has he hurt some passerby?

The knife on the pavement reminds Catiuccia of her fiasco with Stefano; it wounds her heart all over again. Stefano, she knows, is working in Orvieto now, learning the craft of art restoration. She has seen him here and there when he's been home on a weekend, and whenever she has, she's hated him a little, though even she knows she hasn't much right to, and would more than happily accept any attention from him still. Of course there's none.

She stoops and retrieves the knife. She is mildly surprised that it so closely resembles the one she gave to Stefano, the one she picked up on the square those few weeks ago. That a thing so similar should again have come to her by accident seems some faint inkling of fate. She suddenly believes she'll be a real woman soon, perhaps like the lady she noticed from the writing school at the villa just outside the village, the one with the short blond hair, the notebook, the stylish black pants and blouse. It's as though she has her own story to tell.

Catiuccia *should* tell that story. It would involve a knife. She'd have to make everything up, of course. All at once she imagines she could make it up right now, recite it to Ugo, who leans out of his house above her. For the first time, she notices how handsome a boy he is. Has he always been so good to look at? She is especially taken by the dimples that soften his jaw, on which a smudge of beard is just visible.

A story might win him. All she needs now is some "Once upon a time . . ."

III.

Sublime to Rigamarole

Fact, Dream, and Labor

Robert Frost and the New England Attitude

I HAVE A BELOVED NEIGHBOR somewhat south of here, a woman of eighty who lives in the house where she was born. Ruthie had to end her schooling in the eighth grade and go to work. In my family's company, she visited Boston for the only time in her life; she has never seen another city. She is, in short, a provincial in the purely descriptive sense of that term. By this I do not present her as an unfortunate, even if many self-styled, well-coiffed intellectuals might, for in fact this woman is wise in so many important *human* ways that condescension toward her would be the worst kind of arrogance.

In any case, neighbor Ruthie is pure New England, and she has some awareness of poetry: it goes back to the verse that she, like many American children of her time, committed to memory—work by poets like Longfellow or Noyes or Whittier, the so-called schoolroom poets, to whom of course we do seem obliged to condescend, even if they did, after all, command the kind of devotion scarcely imaginable to modern or postmodern writers. Of course there's one obvious exception: Robert Frost, who, while greater than the schoolroomers, enjoyed the last national reputation akin to theirs.

That reputation, to be sure, often rested on misprision of Frost's oeuvre. Not that Frost often sought to correct any misprision: if people chose to see him as a twinkly old Yankee, who might be caught reciting poems while seated on the general store's cracker barrel, he wouldn't necessarily object. Renown, after all, was renown, and the man craved it, in ways that could—as academics have been especially fervid to reveal—now and then make him morally disquieting.

Every cliché, including the one that construes Frost as the cracker-barrel philosopher, the ruggedly independent New Englander, does of course have its germ of truth. That's why I have mentioned Ruthie, with whom I think Frost has an odd commonalty. Let me start by replicating a conversation I lately had with her, after I'd asked her opinion of zoning in her native hamlet. Her part in it went somewhat like this: "Well, some of 'em says it'll be a good thing, and it'll keep the village pretty. But then some of 'em says it'll tie the hands of people who lived here all their lives and want to give a piece of property to their kids or that-like. Then different ones say that hamburger places and silly shops will ruin what we look like. Then others claim there's no stopping progress. I mean to study it, because the truth is, I don't know too much about it."

That is a vivid dramatization of what "independence" really means, the word, etymologically, suggesting that Ruthie's position hangs from no rigidly defined branch on the philosophical or political tree.

My wife once noted that a famous Frost poem could, without undue strain, be translated, as it were, into Ruth-ese. It would begin, "Some of 'em says the world will end in fire, / Some of 'em says in ice," and proceed in the same manner. The upper New England attitude that lies under the poems of Ruthie and Robert is in that implicit demurrer: "I don't know too much about it."

This is not at all to say that with regard to zoning Ruthie knows *nothing* about it, nor with regard to Apocalypse Frost knows nothing. It's that neither party knows "too much." Each wants to think certain crucial matters over so as to know more. The odds are that in the woman's case this'll demand a good deal of effort; in the man's it'll demand a lifetime. In either case, we won't soon hear either party offer an unqualified pronouncement.

This is one of the things that has drawn me to live all my adult life in rural New England, to have become—in the sly and friendly-insulting words of my own general storekeeper—a "neo-native." In a world, especially a literary world, where everyone seems hell bent on expounding a moral or political certainty, I find much to commend in the fundamentally skeptical, and that includes *self*-skeptical, frame of mind I've roughly limned here, one that I encounter every day in my own Vermont hamlet. The cartoon of the independent Yankee shows a flinty man or woman who is full of dogged opinion, but the true Yankee provincial refuses, precisely, to hang his or her hat on a single peg.

I will be speaking, of course, mostly of Frost's poetry, but to begin with, let me trot out a couple of widely accepted generalizations about the man as man. For example, Frost was a political conservative, even a reactionary. Well, yes, I suppose. He was—as may perhaps be seen in an allegory like "Brown's Descent"—against Roosevelt's New Deal. But why? Disagree with his view as you may (I do), but recognize that, like Dr. Williams, he disliked the centralization of government chiefly on the grounds that it was anti-egalitarian, paternalistic, above all patronizing to the poor. To that extent, Frost's core values were, by his time's standards, what we might otherwise call "progressive." Yet I don't mean to fuss about matters political; the real point here is that, as a human being as well as in his capacity as a man of letters, Frost resisted any such labeling throughout his life.

Frost was a sexist. Well, yes, perhaps: people like Jeffrey Myers have taken pains to show how ill he could treat his wife, to indicate that his relationship with Kathleen Morrison was exploitative, and so on. In response, even having conceded all that, I'll merely ask a rhetorical question: could anyone be so shrewd as to *feign* the sympathy and admiration for women that Frost reveals in "A Servant to Servants," "The Hill Wife," "Home Burial," "The Silken Tent," or the sadly underknown "The Wild Grapes"? I'll leave you to read or reread those works and come to your own conclusions, because I don't know too much about it.

I suspect, however, that Frost was like any great man or woman—or rather like any man or woman. He could be almost monstrous and he could be almost unbelievably tender. However all that may be, my real interest here anyway is in Frost's staggering literary accomplishment.

There is an oft-quoted line from *A Boy's Will;* in "Mowing," Frost claims that "The fact is the sweetest dream that labor knows." That line—like "I took the one less traveled by," which I'll presently address in *its* context—is in general reductively understood, if understood at all. Many see in it Frost's radically Enlightenment position: his resistance to the metaphysical and his simultaneous attraction to the empirical; his privileging (as we say nowadays) of fact over speculation, of the immediate over the occult, of the palpable over the oneiric, and so on. And so this sonnet may well be—in one respect. But we must be careful, for Frost is *never* one-dimensional.

There are three abstractions in this famous line: *fact, dream,* and *labor,* and I mean among other things to seek a definition of each term and, more importantly, to suggest how each may relate to the other. Does the line tell us that factuality is the sweetest *thing* that labor knows? Is it the sweetest *reward, pleasure, distraction?* None of the above. No: Frost calls fact the sweetest *dream* that labor knows.

As in virtually all Frost's poems that involve physical or even mental work, it is possible without undue strain to identify labor with the poet's effort to make poems. What is less easy to see is how fact and dream figure into that effort.

MOWING

There was never a sound beside the wood but one,
And that was my long scythe whispering to the ground.
What was it it whispered? I knew not well myself;
Perhaps it was something about the heat of the sun,
Something, perhaps, about the lack of sound—
And that was why it whispered and did not speak.

It was no dream of the gift of idle hours,
Or easy gold at the hand of fay or elf:
Anything more than the truth would have seemed too weak
To the earnest love that laid the swale in rows,
Not without feeble-pointed spikes of flowers
(Pale orchises), and scared a bright green snake.
The fact is the sweetest dream that labor knows.
My long scythe whispered and left the hay to make.

Frost seems firmly to ground himself in the physical, factual world. And yet he can't resist thinking that the sound of his scythe is eloquent of . . . what? "I knew not well myself," he says, as one might say, again, "I don't know too much about it." In the ninth line, the conventional "turn" of the sonnet form that he deliberately chooses, the poet suggests what he's after: "Anything more than the truth would have seemed too weak."

But as much as the line sounds like a clarification, it must give us pause: what, say, would be more than truth? What about it would constitute a weakening, and a weakening of what? Frost tellingly appears to dismiss the notion of the revelatory, let alone the apocalyptic, which, after all, might have wrongly entered the eager reader's consciousness when he or she beheld a lone figure with a scythe. He also dismisses the mythology of literary Romance: "It was no dream of the gift of idle hours, / Or easy gold at the hand of fay or elf." (In his musings on "the heat of the sun," he may also be recalling the song late in *Cymbeline,* and in the bargain slyly suggesting the inadequacy of even his greatest forebear.)

Yet it seems important to me that, even if he claims to discard them, these supra-mundane associations are the ones that immediately leap to Frost's speaker's mind as he mows. Even as the mower turns, in the sestet, to the "earnest love" he wants to associate with his labor; even as he tries, precisely, to bring the reader, too bent perhaps on allegory, down to the quotidian, he cannot utterly banish those transcendental, *non-*factual associations from his mind. If we note the Edenic proximity of his own innocent presence to that of a bright green snake, we can, I believe, hardly be accused of mere symbol-mongering.

So what can we make of what had seemed an authoritative utterance, "The fact is the sweetest dream that labor knows"? We can make either very little of it, or more than we can quickly and conveniently handle. At any rate, we must recognize that, in his labor, Frost all but inevitably—here and elsewhere—figures *fact as dream* and *dream as fact.* He warns us that higher callings and earthly ones resist facile distinctions, even his own. (Consider, say, "Two Tramps in Mudtime," which appeared more than twenty years later than "Mowing," in which the speaker avers that "My object in living is to unite / My avocation and my vocation".)

Frost, I might claim, however outrageously in light of his alleged Enlightenment stance, his anti-Romanticism, is our century's purest embodiment of what Keats called "negative capability," the capacity to be of more than one mind in any given moment or even lifetime. That capacity, in Keats's own words, enables its possessor to "be in uncertainties and doubts without any irritable reaching after fact and reason." This is not to say that Frost doesn't reach after fact at all. Rather, the gesture is not "irritable" but inquiring.

Like Keats, Frost will not, indeed cannot simply put an end to his uncertainty—or his reader's. He makes his exit from the hayfield, but his scythe is still saying something that resists pure closure: "My long scythe whispered and left the hay to make." It is not he, Frost, who does the whispering here, nor he who leaves the hay to season; it's the scythe, whose very eloquence he has been trying, unsuccessfully, to decipher from the start.

As it turns out, fact and the supra-factual are invariably intertwined in this author's opus. The transcendent exists there in spades, but it always emerges in concert with keen and patient physical observation. That concatenation of the empirical and the abstract, I submit, is a measure of Frost's greatness, and stands—incidentally—as a model to any author who aspires to greatness of his or her own. We can understand what recognizable factual components give rise to Frost's more abstract speculations; we are grounded before we take off.

This grounding is one of the things, also, that helped Frost toward the reputation he did so singularly enjoy. Because of it, anyone—from kindergartener to academic specialist—can get at least *something* out of virtually any Frost poem on first reading or hearing. The something gotten may simply be a turn of phrase: "And miles to go before I sleep," "Something there is that doesn't love a wall," "Nature's first green is gold," "Better to go down dignified," "What to make of a diminished thing," on and on. It's one testimony to Frost's genius indeed that so many people out there, even some who claim to dislike poetry, can assemble their own small anthologies of Frostian phrases, almost as many, I'd wager, as of Shakespeare phrases. We feel, in a sense, somehow invited in by Frost, just as we—or at least I—too often feel invited out by an Ezra Pound or even a Wallace Stevens, to say nothing of contemporaries like John Ashbery or Anne Carson.

The something gotten may also, as I've said, represent misprision, though it's more likely to be *partial* misprision, a lapse into that always erroneous assumption of one-dimensionality. Remember, "Some of 'em says this, some of 'em that." Frost is an independent Yankee in a sense more profound than the cliché implies. He never knows *too* much about a given issue. He is a seeker, and, as such, he invites us—nay, requires us—to be seekers ourselves, to aspire to knowing, as he says in the poem so called "For Once, Then, Something." A modest agenda, it seems, but actually a lot harder than it sounds.

Fact and dream, the physical and the speculative, perpetually coexist in Frost's seeking, and he urges us to see that coexistence not merely as a hallmark of his work but also as a condition of human life. We too must ponder the relations of the rational and the supra-rational, the practical and the emotional; we must likewise understand the perils of becoming schematic in our ponderings of these apparent opposites. "A foolish consistency is the hobgoblin of little minds," said one of Frost's few New England peers; by virtue of that axiom alone, it is unsurprising that Frost, often very stingy with his praise of other authors, should have been fairly steady in his esteem for Emerson.

In a two-line poem at midcareer, Frost wrote that "We dance around in a ring and suppose, / But the Secret sits in the middle and knows." That is a not very good, indeed an almost annoyingly cute little couplet, to be sure; yet we can infer Yankee skepticism from it, no? Well, yes, we can—provided we understand that Frost is likewise skeptical of skepticism itself, or of any rigid position. As he says in another short poem of the same vintage, "I love to toy with the Platonic notion / That wisdom need not be of Athens Attic, / But well may be Laconic, even Boeotian. / At least I will not have it systematic."

The poet's distrust of systems might render his work persistently vexing, frustrating, were he not, coincidentally, a genius. How a genius? Well, beyond his brilliant control of form and prosody (on which I could write, indeed have, other essays), his work is rich in the degree to which the author's urge to transcendence checks his commitment to the factual *without entirely canceling it,* just as his urge to turn himself "to earthward" checks but doesn't entirely negate the transcendental impulse. Again, I think of his great predecessor Keats's notion of negative capability. Frost is to that extent endlessly complex, whereas a contemporary of his like Pound is, in my view, merely complicated.

One cannot, for example, use Frost as a proof of any one attitude's accuracy or moral cleanliness (or, as too many academic snoops seem to wish, moral *un*-cleanliness). Frost insists that it's you, Dear Reader, who must—if you will—come to fixed conclusions on your own. The author simply refuses to do so.

I mean now to look, if briefly, at a number of poems, most of them well known, from the perspective, or really the non-perspective I've sought to present up until now. Let's start with one of the most famous:

THE ROAD NOT TAKEN

Two roads diverged in a yellow wood,
And sorry I could not travel both
And be one traveler, long I stood
And looked down one as far as I could
To where it bent in the undergrowth;

Then took the other, as just as fair,
And having perhaps the better claim,
Because it was grassy and wanted wear;
Though as for that, the passing there
Had worn them really about the same,

And both that morning equally lay
In leaves no step had trodden black.
Oh, I kept the first for another day!
Yet knowing how way leads on to way,
I doubted if I should ever come back.

I shall be telling this with a sigh,
Somewhere ages and ages hence:
Two roads diverged in a wood, and I—
I took the one less traveled by,
And that has made all the difference.

Though there are other candidates, this may be the most glibly interpreted Frost poem of all, the one on which more than any other hangs the clichéd version of his Yankee individualism, which can quickly become a cliché of undaunted self-actualization, which can in turn be used as a guide to up-from-your bootstraps conservatism or—when part of it is borrowed for the title, say, of a popular self-help book—as the working motto of the New Age bliss patrollers. In any case, at graduation ceremonies, retirement dinners, and other more or less formal events, we find good old Robert striking out on his own, God bless him. And we find him there despite the author's insistence that there's anything but a radical difference between the path he takes and the one more traveled by. Indeed, as the poem very explicitly indicates, the two roads are "really about the same."

I've forgotten the provenance of a telling letter, but in it Frost suggests to a friend that "not one in ten will see the humor" of "The Road

Not Taken." What sort of humor? Well, the humor of a put-on, in which the poet melodramatizes himself and his choice, and, again, acknowledges as much on the very page. He has a vision, a true one, of his later vamping off this poem: "I shall be saying this with a sigh, / Somewhere ages and ages hence." That is, I'll play the cracker-barrel philosopher, the rugged individualist, and people, amazingly, will buy the whole charade.

But of course it is not charade alone. If we discover what Frost called humor here, we must, predictably, find the serious note too. Frost did, after all, opt for a different road from the one traveled by his contemporaries. Pound and Eliot had left the United States for Europe. Frost came home from there. Williams became a free-verse propagandist. Frost stuck to the measure. Those others located themselves in great metropolitan zones. On return from England, Frost settled in remote mountain territory.

So although our poet tempts us to see his choice as all but arbitrary, he *simultaneously* tempts us to see it as deeply consequential. He asks, then, whether we can be "systematic" in our reading (and by extension our lives) even if we want to be; he asks whether any decision can be purely genuine *or* purely contrived. Aren't our choices inevitably something of both? Does not our cleaving to fact and physicality inevitably lead us to dream and vision? Do not dream and vision restore us to the factual and physical?

He is a Casbah of a poet, this fellow, and no matter the issue or instance, we can never absolutely learn our way around. We must keep backing and filling, and asking directions from his poems, which seem to help us out—except that they always send us back on our rounds. This is, I believe, what makes Frost inexhaustible.

Let's look at another almost equally well-known poem, "Mending Wall." "Something there is that doesn't love a wall," it begins, and years ago clever people understood that one of the things to dislike such barriers is—frost. And indeed, feeling, as he says, some mischief in himself, the human Frost wonders aloud to his neighbor whether it wouldn't be mutually good to destroy the wall, to "want it down."

We are all primed, maybe, to be a bit New Age ourselves, to assume that social contrivances are injurious to our species, that we must eliminate the walls between one person and another. If the wall-building partner says, twice, that "Good fences make good neighbors," he must be that stereotypical Yankee individualist, a hidebound old crank who deliberately and perversely smothers communication, revelation of the inner child, the dreamer, and whatever else.

But mischief doesn't prevent Frost from continuing to build, he on one side, the neighbor on the other. And note how he ends his poem by presenting that same backward neighbor in an ambiguous visionary condition, the visionary once more arising from, inseparable from, the factual. Yet it *is* a vision:

> I see him there,
> Bringing a stone grasped firmly from the top
> In each hand, like an old-stone savage armed.
> He moves in darkness, as it seems to me.

Ah yes, we may think, the old man is nothing short of benighted, even savage, darkness his element. And yet that darkness is

> Not of woods only and the shade of trees.
> He will not go behind his father's saying,
> And he likes having thought of it so well
> He says again, "Good fences make good neighbors."

If on the one hand we may uncomplimentarily see this rough New Englander as of the Stone Age—as surely Frost does—we must also recognize in the neighbor—as Frost likewise does—a kind of primordial figure, one whose ritual behavior and allegiance to the word of his father (and all his father's fathers) have enabled him to endure in a hardscrabble place. That endurance, we should note, as the poet may already have foreseen, would prove to be more than Frost could command himself. The "good fences/good neighbors" saw may be primitive, but it's also one of the tricks that wise elders have used from time immemorial as they stuck it out in Frost's ungenerous landscape.

In "Mending Wall," derision, awe, condescension, and admiration all exist cheek by jowl. But such bizarre coalescences abound everywhere in Frost's poetry. It is unsurprising that so apparently fierce a proponent of "the fact" finds himself everywhere at least partly foiled. "Birches" is another good example. The poet, when he sees "birches bend to left and right," explains to us the burden placed upon those trees by ice storms. That seems the simple, factual truth, but Frost portrays himself as impatient with his own factuality: "But I was going to say when Truth broke in / With all her matter of fact about the ice-storm. . . ."

What *was* he going to say? He tells us that rather than factual truth he prefers vision, in this instance of a backcountry boy "too far from town to learn baseball, / Whose only play was what he found himself, / Summer or winter, and could play alone." (Once more, the physical gesture, the boy's playful "labor," can easily be compared to Frost's own solitary work as poet.)

The author is wistful about having been a swinger of birches himself, and so he dreams of going back to be one again. When and why? As I have noted elsewhere,

> It's when I'm weary of considerations,
> And life is too much like a pathless wood
> Where your face burns and tickles with the cobwebs
> Broken across it, and one eye is weeping
> From a twig's having lashed across it open.

In this condition, he'd "like to get away from Earth awhile." And he'd

> like to go by climbing a birch tree,
> And climb black branches up a snow-white trunk
> Toward heaven, till the tree could bear no more,
> But dipped its top and set me down again.
> That would be good both going and coming back.
> One could do worse than be a swinger of birches.

And indeed that's just what he is in his labor, a poet who aspires to the super-earthly even as he recognizes, in the same poem, that "Earth's the right place for love: / I don't know where it's likely to go better." That is, "I don't know too much about it."

I'll read one more full poem, a brilliant and mind-bending sonnet, and then come to my appropriately inconclusive conclusion.

DESIGN

> I found a dimpled spider, fat and white,
> On a white heal-all, holding up a moth
> Like a white piece of rigid satin cloth—
> Assorted characters of death and blight
> Mixed ready to begin the morning right,
> Like the ingredients of a witches' broth—
> A snow-drop spider, a flower like froth,
> And dead wings carried like a paper kite.
>
> What had that flower to do with being white,
> The wayside blue and innocent heal-all?
> What brought the kindred spider to that height,
> Then steered the white moth thither in the night?
> What but design of darkness to appall?—
> If design govern in a thing so small.

As always, Frost has clearly observed the simple facts, then transcribed them with utter accuracy. But of course they turn out to be anything but simple, maybe anything but facts. How can the blue heal-all have become white? How can the predator spider and the dead moth be "kindred"? Is this a chance encounter or, as the pun suggests, a "rite"? And so on. Frost asks these apparently rhetorical questions and several others, all designed to question the nature of design itself.

What was the force behind such arresting oddity as he encounters here? Frost's first answer seems authoritative, "What but design of darkness to appall?" Yet that answer appears straightforward only until we realize that it's not so at all, that the very word "appall," for example, means among other things "to make white," so the answer may be read as "What but design of darkness to make white?" We might take that as a consoling line: things aren't as black and gloomy as they seem. Or we can apply a more conventional use of the verb, in which case the scene is *only* appalling. Or we can do both, and can go on pondering such ultimates.

The concluding couplet throws us off-balance too. "What but design of darkness to appall? / If design govern in a thing so small." Maybe we should have done with our hifalutin teleology and get back to the factual: it's just a spider, just a flower, just a moth. That'll at least make things easier, no? Yet is it really a relief to us, the notion that this little death-drama is merely the sort of thing that happens to happen, and nothing more? Are we truly happier to know that there exists no inclusive design at all in the world? Is that notion preferable to one that sees some operative, overarching scheme, even a malign one?

Again, Frost makes us ask these questions of *ourselves*. If we crave design, if we crave the systematic, then we'd better work it out on our own. He'll raise the issues, but he won't offer naked opinion. As my friend Ruthie might put it: "Some of 'em says there's design; different ones says there ain't. I don't know too much about it."

An obliquely related anecdote: Several years ago, our pastor Malcolm Grobe preached a sermon one Sunday. Ruthie had come along to church with my family that morning. Malcolm's sermon was brilliant and difficult: it had to do with how a Christian might envision heaven; like a Frost poem, it raised all manner of issues, some of which seemed to contravene others. It was the best sort of sermon, simultaneously a challenge both to doubt and to faith.

As I drove Ruthie home I asked her how she'd liked the service. She said it had been very fine, especially that sermon. "The minister, he meant to vex us," she said, with obvious approval. *To vex*. It's a fairly rare locution in the contemporary lexicon, but it seemed just right to me then. One of the things I love about the New Englanders of Ruthie's generation is the way in which that generation's talk retains these vestiges of the north country language that Frost himself knew and used. One says "to want" for "to need," say, as in "That door wants a new hinge." One eats a "lunch" at any time of day, a lunch being simply a light meal. One is more inclined to a "surmise" than to an "idea," and so on.

The fragility of such language is patent in the era of email, cable TV, virtual reality, and the rest, when our language is increasingly shrunken and flattened out, when it's geographically indistinct. For whatever reason, then, I am sentimental about that more copious and colorful talk; it may be one of the things that would make me sentimental about Frost even if his gifts were not so prodigious as to make mere sentimentality irrelevant.

In any case, like my minister's sermon, Frost's poetry does indeed "vex." And, as I've tried to suggest, it does so on purpose. Consider, a propos, the matter of this poet's religion. It was there, I am all but certain, but to understand it would be almost as hard as understanding God's will itself. But it is precisely the *effort* at understanding that Frost summons us to. Such effort—religious or otherwise—to make the world cohere will be relentless and, doubtless, inconclusive this side of the grave. One of Frost's New England heirs seems to know as much. In a famous assertion at the end of a famous poem, Richard Wilbur writes that "Love calls us to the things of this world." Easy enough, right? Well, as Ruthie would say, and I join Wilbur in saying, "I don't know too much about it."

NOTE

This essay was originally presented as a talk in Franconia, New Hampshire, on that state's Robert Frost Day.

On Keats's "To Autumn"

AT MANY A READING IN OUR TIME, this or that author will introduce a given poem in a way that can put me off. The words will vary, but the gist is generally as follows: "I notice something here that you too might have noticed . . . if only you were as sensitive as I, which of course you're not."

In these pages, I think I've shown my distaste for the idea that poets possess some supranormal sensitivity. That idea has never sold well with me (especially when used to defend awful behavior). Thus, though he does so in one of my favorite works, I wince a bit at Wordworth's claim: "We poets in our youth begin in gladness; / But thereof come in the end despondency and madness." I doubt this truth—if a truth at all—applies any more to poets than to others.

I'll ignore more egregious claims from some of my contemporaries, mentioning all this only because John Keats was crucial in bringing me to what is, I hope, a more modest attitude. And he still corrects of the self-vaunting in which I like anyone can indulge as man and author.

I first read Keats when I was a college boy, who may unconsciously have dreamed of being a writer. But beforehand I'd gotten addicted, precisely, to Wordsworth. I was more or less innocent of canonical poetic history, so the idea that epic or romance energies might inhere in the ordinary, and thus be available to anybody, including me, felt at once like a revelation and even a permission.

And a relief: I was also addicted to the blues tradition in American music, and now I could believe, for example, that the image of sexual infidelity in Muddy Waters's "Long Distance Call"—*another mule is kickin' in your stall*—rooted as it was in acute observation of the commonplace, qualified as poetry. If people challenged me, I'd cite this or that passage from Wordsworth's poems or his prefaces to *Lyrical Ballads*.

Trouble was, the more Wordsworth I read, the more my night thoughts: Why should this proponent of the quotidian himself seem persistently . . . well, so highfalutin?

I mean, an epic subtitled "The Growth of a Poet's Mind"? Come on!

Needless to say, my understanding of Wordsworth's efforts was imperfect at best; yet the poet seemed to premonish the attitude I disparaged on beginning these thoughts: Watch my mind grow, and your own little mind might grow an inch or so in the process.

Now, still convinced that in most ways Wordsworth remains the greater figure, I'm actually less apt to take him up of an evening than I am the author who said in a February 1818 letter to John Reynolds that

> Wordsworth &c should have their due from us but for the sake of a few fine imaginative or domestic passages, are we to be bullied into a certain Philosophy engendered in the whims of an Egotist[?]

This is the Keats who, in another letter to Reynolds, wrote that by every germ of Spirit sucking the Sap from mould ethereal every human might become great, and Humanity instead of being a wide heath of Furse and Briars with here and there a remote Oak or Pine, would become a grand democracy of Forest Trees.

Keats at his best would shun the more-sensitive-than-thou posture, and for my money his best showed up in "To Autumn," whose most affecting lines for me weren't the celebrated closing ones but those at the start of section II:

> Who hath not seen thee oft amid thy store?
> Sometimes whoever seeks abroad may find
> Thee sitting careless on a granary floor. . . .

Though the poet has seen the goddess, he suggests that everyone who has made the least effort knows her too. The idea delighted me: if the great Keats were just another onlooker, then the other onlookers— including me—were conceivably poets too, *in potentia*.

And yet, from my later perspective, the very issue of greatness seems progressively dismantled by the poem in question. Yes, "whoever seeks abroad" is a prospective artist, a vessel for the imagination, but "To Autumn" makes even more radical claims. Not only does it dismiss individual greatness as an important aim, but it also deemphasizes the importance of individuality itself. From the moment just cited, the author's own ego progressively cedes itself to something far broader (in this case, the landscape), Keats suggesting that the numinous really *can* inhere in the ordinary, perhaps without great exercise of will on anyone's part.

The willful writer, the would-be prophet of a work like *The Fall of Hyperion,* seems to recognize (and not just for "literary" reasons—recall the rapid decline in Keats's health by September of the great year), now sees the inutility of prophetic aspiration.

Note at the start that Autumn is simply addressed as a natural phenomenon, however multifaceted. Though several of the 1819 odes are similar in this way, most do contain classical allusions or quasi-allusions. "To Autumn" consistently eschews them. Indeed, stanza 1 being a grammatical fragment, authorial comment on the season is truncated; the only active wills are those of the "conspiring" sun and the "thinking" bees.

Stanza 2 continues the theme of poetic vision's omni-availability. It's not until the start of the final stanza that we find the old prophet's ego intruding, however subtly and briefly: "Where are the songs of spring?" Keats asks, no doubt recalling his own odes of a few months earlier. But he rallies himself: "Think not of them, thou hast thy music too." The poet joins the company of all seekers abroad, addressing himself in the second person.

If that last surmise seems overwrought, note that after the minimal intrusion of ego, Keats becomes increasingly descriptive, even "imagist." So far from being prophecy, "To Autumn" in its closure is not even testimony. It isn't Keats, for example, who laments the fact that *he* is dying; it's the *day* that is. It isn't he who mourns the demise of the day and year; "small gnats" do. The "full-grown lambs" don't mourn at all but simply "bleat."

We've moved away from pathetic fallacy, pathos itself—largely a human construct, even in the portraiture of insects—draining from the poem as it ebbs. If "bleat" struck us as a predictable verb to apply to sheep, hear how generic and colloquial the remaining verbs in the ode sound, crickets merely *singing,* the redbreast *whistling,* swallows *twittering.* The prevailing vocabulary in the final passage's dramatic components—the verbs—is as common as any observer's might be. So much, the author implies, even for a poet's superior attunement to language.

In a song of spring, the "Ode to Psyche," Keats could write:

> So let me be thy choir, and make a moan
> Upon the midnight hours;
> Thy voice, thy lute, thy pipe, thy incense sweet
> From swinging censer teeming;
> Thy shrine, thy grove, thy oracle, thy heat
> Of pale-mouth'd prophet dreaming.

Now his ego's vatic aspirations surrender to something well outside the ego: in the third stanza's vision of nature, even brutes and bugs have as much right to voice themselves as a bard.

And yet, even as he downplays the issue of greatness and prophecy,

Keats leaves us "To Autumn," itself an undeniably great poem. We may be up against a paradox, though the author himself might see this September song less as great than beautiful, to choose a ubiquitous Keatsian term.

The power of "To Autumn" stems, paradoxically, from its modesty—and from its democratic impulse. And so long as we are stuck on paradox, the ode may show our anti-prophet to be prophetic after all. Ours is an era often sneered at for producing so many poets but so few great ones. If, however, a progressively democratic spirit is to attend the unfolding of human history (and mustn't we believe it will, if we're to sustain hope?), perhaps the era is the one forecast by Keats in his letter to Reynolds. Maybe a collective expression of beauty will sustain us. Maybe we should take heart from the many voices that are chanting their way into the so-called canon.

Maybe our poetry—as Keats put it in the early "Sleep and Poetry"—will "be a friend / To soothe the cares, and lift the thoughts of man." And woman too. And all humanity.

Wordsworth and His "Michael"

The Pastor Passes

> If from the public way you turn your steps
> Up the tumultuous brook of Green-head Ghyll,
> You will suppose that with an upright path
> Your feet must struggle; in such bold ascent
> The pastoral mountains front you, face to face.
> But, courage! for around that boisterous brook
> The mountains have all opened out themselves,
> And made a hidden valley of their own.
> No habitation can be seen; but they
> Who journey thither find themselves alone
> With a few sheep, with rocks and stones, and kites
> That overhead are sailing in the sky.
> It is in truth an utter solitude;
> Nor should I have made mention of this Dell
> But for one object which you might pass by,
> Might see and notice not. Beside the brook
> Appears a straggling heap of unhewn stones!

I'm going to assume here that those seventeen lines from the often neglected induction of Wordsworth's "Michael" prefigure the concern of the poem at large, which is Wordsworth's desire to transmit a pastoral legacy—one he fears we may spurn.

The poet begins by assuring us from experience that, despite the bleakness we confront, "courage" will have its reward. Though we might ignorantly "pass by" the central object of Wordsworth's enthusiasm, we can with his guidance avail ourselves of a special prize: the "straggling heap of unhewn stones!"

Why the exclamation point? The rhetorical vehemence where none seems appropriate is our first clue that the writer anticipates indifference, asks us to bear with him until he can justify the importance of an observation that may strike us as trivial. What interest, we could ask, is here, in a place without human habitation?

Wordsworth's induction is quite literally a leading-in, geographic and thematic, but the urgency in its tone signals his anxiety lest we feel led astray. The place is hidden, he would tell us, but that is not to say that it is barren. The poet calls such emphatic attention to the rock pile primarily because it suggests a tale, whose value he insists upon.

Stephen Parrish has traced the development of this narrative from early balladic fragments to the blank-verse rendition of the 1800 *Lyrical Ballads*. Interestingly, what remains of the "ballad-Michael" is largely parodic, although its apparent theme is if anything *more* pathetic than that of the well-known "Michael." Parrish notes the ballad's "jocular qualities," but indicates that

> they are qualities that Wordsworth, for better or worse, outgrew as he moved toward the lyric styles of his later years, and the somber philosophical mode of the *Prelude* and the *Excursion*. As much as any other single event, the conversion of the anapestic "ballad-Michael" into a muted blank-verse narrative signalizes Wordsworth's movement in 1800 away from his early experimental voices into the main region of his song.[1]

I find in this change of tone a modification of Wordsworth's poetico-historical sense. The relative seriousness of the ultimate "Michael" shows that by 1800 he considered himself vigorously engaged in the "sustained eighteenth-century debate over the nature and value of pastoral poetry."[2]

There can be little doubt as to where Wordsworth stood, outwardly, in this debate. He must have imagined the censoriousness to which a Samuel Johnson would have submitted his shepherd's tale, even as he sought to refute it. Man confined to the country, we may remember from *Rambler* 36, "can be shewn but seldom in such circumstances as attract curiosity," let alone sympathy.

From the start, Wordsworth was determined to counter this sort of opinion. Yet I think the jocularity of the "ballad-Michael" indicates early doubt in the poet himself about the pastoral. The lighter elements of the initial narrative fragments were imaginably self-parodying: though he had a moving tale to tell, the author's doggerel-like anapests betrayed unease about its setting and its characters. This uneasiness marked, so to speak, an inward relation to the eighteenth-century debate on pastoral.

Writing his final draft of "Michael" in the face of a sustained critical suspicion, Wordsworth's public defense of pastoralism grew more intense. Still, the opening passage of the poem remains ambivalent in its relation to the pastoral issue; the self-doubt of the "ballad-Michael" carries into the finished narrative, and no outward assurance can expel the interior unsettledness.

Again, to the induction:

> Beside the brook
> Appears a straggling heap of unhewn stones!
> And to that simple story appertains
> A story—unenriched with strange events,
> Yet not unfit, I deem, for the fireside,
> Or for the summer shade. It was the first
> Of those domestic tales that spake to me
> Of Shepherds, dwellers in the valleys, men
> Whom I already loved. . . .

Wordsworth feels his authority to "deem" the prospective tale a worthy one, if only because it is intimately bound up with the rural and commonplace, which he had decided to take as his purview. It is not necessary that the poet dress his setting up, add anything fanciful to it; the place remains "unenriched with strange events," meaning less that it is impoverished than that it needs no embellishment. Its very value lies in the fact that it contains obvious things; to that extent it contravenes Augustan distaste for pastoral, or, equally injurious, Augustan insistence that pastoral be at least refined, idealized.

Wordsworth means to show a pure unself-consciousness about sharing domestic tales or tales of shepherds, in fact singling "Michael" out as the first of such tales that he ever heard. It is thus his archetypal story of low and rustic life: at ease with this one, he will be at ease with any of his pastoral poems.

And yet, although the exclamatory reference to the stone pile portends something fabulous and strange, the poet's subsequent announcement that his narrative is "*un*enriched with strange events" slightly qualifies the portent. The language of the opening seventeen lines stresses the importance of this locale and the tale associated with it, but the rhetoric seems modest. Indeed Wordsworth will not actively defend "Michael"'s instructional value; he quietly claims instead that the poem is "*not unfit* . . . for the fireside / Or for the summer shade."

The vacillation in tone—from magisterial to self-effacing—runs throughout Wordsworth's induction, and invites scrutiny. Again, we've been told that the story of "Michael" captivated Wordsworth the child because it spoke of the very shepherds whom he loved. He loved them, however,

> not verily
> For their own sakes, but for the fields and hills
> Where was their occupation and abode.
> And hence this Tale, while I was yet a boy,
> Careless of books, yet having felt the power
> Of Nature, by the gentle agency
> Of natural objects, led me on to feel
> For passions that were not my own, and think
> (At random and imperfectly indeed)
> On man, the heart of man, and human life.

Presumably, the mature poet has appropriated the important "passions" which were dim to the child; he can now think purposively, perhaps almost "perfectly," on the human condition, as is implied by the final line here. But the conclusion of the induction permits the same double reading as its opening:

> Therefore, although it be a history
> Homely and rude, I will relate the same
> For the delight of a few natural hearts,
> And, with yet fonder feeling, for the sake
> Of youthful poets, who among these hills,
> Will be my second self when I am gone.

Apparent assurance is again qualified by some apology. Not that the words "homely" and "rude" necessarily constitute such apology, since in Wordsworth's work at large they tend to be honorific; and yet, like "unenriched," they may. The real discomfort here is in the sense of an audience contracted from "a few natural hearts" to "youthful poets"—from few hearers to fewer still. This is unsettling, because the induction, *like the tale itself*, involves the effort of a father-figure to pass on an inheritance to a "second self," in Wordsworth's case a collective one. Michael will explain to *his* heir that "these fields were burthened when they came to me." Similarly, Wordsworth's "fields," his commitment to "low" pastoral, came to him burdened—by neglect, or Johnsonian ridicule, or Augustan "enrichment."

We're to know that Wordsworth has labored to redeem the pastoral, partly so he may pass it on to younger poets. Yet how many of them are there, and how interested will they be in accepting the bequest? It is sadly relevant that Wordsworth's induction both offers a legacy and prefaces a narrative of *failed* legacy. The poet anticipates Hartley Coleridge's cartoon of him, a generation later, as "A bard whom there were none to praise / And very few to read."

While Wordsworth overtly insists, as Michael implicitly does, that pastoral is a crucial antidote to the ravages of modern life, the unsettling thrust-and-parry of the prologue's tone, combined with Wordsworth's sense of a diminishing group of heirs, suggests the persistence of the poet's inner doubt. He hopes that he has (in both senses) "natural" inheritors, whom he encourages to carry on his work. Yet he seems at times almost to deflect them from so doing, as if himself suspicious of the perdurability of the low and rustic, the "homely" and "rude." "Michael" may be (to swerve from Harold Bloom) a case of the anxiety of influenc*ing:* Wordsworth is fearful of his own redemption of the pastoral, because it may come at a historical moment that makes it feckless. The trees are being cut down, the pastures ruined. The Industrial Revolution is here, and it can't be wished away.

Wordsworth's poetry, therefore, and especially this "pastoral poem," is conceivably original, vis-à-vis the English neglect of true pastoral, and reactionary, vis-à-vis the march of history. Hence the two questions embedded in both prologue and tale—Will there be heirs to the pastoral mode? and, How will their inheritance serve them? In all his poems and prefaces, Wordsworth may seem to answer these with pure confidence; but surely to bequeath "Michael," a story of barren legacy, is to temper that confidence.

The deterioration of Michael's fields, the disappearance of Michael himself and his way of life—these trigger in Wordsworth a perceptible worry that historical or providential forces will overpower his effort to revive and transmit pastoral vision. Quite simply, the younger nature-poet ("among these hills") is to the author as Luke is to Michael: a natural successor, a second self. Both pastor and poet want to keep the land intact, but as Geoffrey Hartman has noticed, the land does not hold Luke, so that the poet is actually Michael's true heir."[3] Wordsworth—sharing Michael's dedication to the perpetuity of rural life—fulfills that covenant which Luke has sundered; the poet after all stresses his attraction to the heap of stones, which is the very symbol of the pastoral contract.

Yet Wordsworth's proprietary contract with the land is complex. At first glance he is palpably suited to be Michael's second self. Early description of the old shepherd might easily fit into a poem like the *Prelude* as *self*-description. The poet has, like Michael,

> been alone
> Amid the heart of many thousand mists,
> That came to him, and left him, on the heights. . . .

But the passage continues:

And grossly that man errs, who should suppose
That the green valleys, and the streams and rocks,
Were things indifferent to the shepherd's thoughts.

Grossly that man errs who questions the old man's deep emotional bond to his environs. Again, the vehemence here seems unwarranted because aprioristic: Wordsworth's anticipation of the reader's "error" intensifies his own identification with the title character. Defending Michael, the poet defends himself. What better legacy, he challenges, than the one contained in their shared pastoral vision?

But Wordsworth may himself be the victim of error, delusion. Comparing these hills and fields to a book which preserves the memory of pastoral ministry, Wordsworth sees in Michael's relation to nature a "linking to [his] acts the certainty of honourable gain." As the story develops, though, Michael will look back and lament "so *little gain* from threescore years."

Wordsworth's public crusade for the poetry of low and rustic life is at least partly undercut by his fear that he may be passing on an unserviceable legacy. The poet may be Michael's true heir, but who will be the poet's heirs?

These psychologistic speculations seem less bald if we consider a fact in the narrative that few have confronted: namely, the falsity of Michael's dilemma as regards the land's forfeiture. Why, rather than dispatching Luke, does the father not permit him to work the land, to save it, as he himself has done against similar obstacles? Bearing in mind the identification of main character and poet, we see that, if literally false, the pastor's dilemma is metaphorically real. Having striven to save the land, to make it "free" of a spreading industrial stain, Michael awakes to find that, oblivious to his striving, the world of capital and credit has simply reversed his labor.

The forfeiture itself, never very clearly detailed, mocks the shepherd's certainty of honorable gain. His emotional investments, the values in which he has believed instinctively, even "blindly," face bankruptcy. The crisis sends the old man into confusion, for it apparently permits no dignified resolution.

Assuming that the correlation between Michael's perplexity and Wordsworth's makes historical sense, I will defer it to look at the relation between Michael and Luke and at that metaphorical reality of the father's bind.

The boy, we are told, is dear to the aged shepherd "less from instinctive tenderness . . . / . . . that blindly works in the hearts of all,"

Than that a child, more than all other gifts
That earth can offer to declining man,
Brings hope with it, and forward-looking thoughts,
And stirrings of inquietude, when they
By tendency of nature needs must fail.

Michael's connection to Luke is unlike that to the land, precisely in *not* being blind—the father has a design on the boy, whom Wordsworth significantly describes as a gift from the earth. Michael, in his decline, looks forward like the poet to a second self; but even the father's earliest behavior toward his heir is complicated. It shows, so to say, a maternal aspect:

> oftentimes
> Old Michael, while [Luke] was a babe in arms,
> Had done him female service, not alone
> For pastime and delight, as is the use
> Of fathers, but with patient mind enforced
> To acts of tenderness; and he had rocked
> His cradle, as with a woman's hand.

Though here a nurse-like generosity prevails, we are reminded that it is "enforced," not instinctive. Michael, pressed by "hope" *and* "inquietude," calculates his womanly pose.

He is, however, more in character, to use Wordsworth's own simplism, when his behavior is manly. Such is the case between Luke's fifth and eighteenth years. But we must avoid simplism ourselves:

> In a later time, ere yet the boy
> Had put on boy's attire, did Michael love,
> Albeit of a stern unbending mind,
> To have the Young-one in his sight, when he
> Wrought in the field, or on his shepherd's stool
> Sate with a fettered sheep before him stretched
> Under the large old oak, that near his door
> Stood single, and, from matchless depths of shade,
> Chosen for the Shearer's covert from the sun,
> Thence in our rustic dialect was called
> THE CLIPPING TREE, a name which yet it bears.
> There, while they two were sitting in the shade,
> With others round them, earnest all and blithe,
> Would Michael exercise his heart with looks
> Of fond correction and reproof bestowed
> Upon the Child, if he disturbed the sheep. . . .

Michael is "exercised," for Wordsworth's passage describes a rite of passage, the point at which Michael initiates Luke into a living and literal pastoral mode. Hence we witness an act both of love and of "a stern unbending mind." The shepherd's affection is checked by chastisement, by "fond correction" in the poet's near-oxymoron. The scene, though "blithe," is also "earnest."

Michael's earnestness, his urgency, is evident in all details—the boy, despite his dress, is scarce even a boy, much less a man. The tending of the sheep is immensely serious, ritualistic, and the ritual's lesson is: Learn, but Do Not Disturb. Luke is exhorted to understand pastoralism, enjoined not to sport with it.

We must return to the link to Wordsworth, who has come to regard himself as guide to, and perhaps even father of an English pastoral, which he means to pass on. The prospect causes his heart, like his main character's, to be "born again," but he may also like Michael simultaneously regard his envisioned, collective successor-self as

> to his office prematurely called,
> . . . .
> Something between a hindrance and a help;
> And for this cause not always, I believe,
> Receiving from his father hire of praise. . . .

Of course, unlike Michael, Wordsworth has no specific and nameable heir in mind. But our conflation of the two men may explain why the crisis for the shepherd comes when Luke, properly initiated, does indeed become the mature second self that the shepherd had desired. In connecting shepherd and poet, we should not so much stress their diffidence in their heirs, real though it is, as their diffidence in their own preparation of the inheritance.

A heavy-hearted Michael concludes that Luke shall leave. The initial effect is relief.

>   "Well, Isabel! this scheme
> These two days, has been meat and drink to me.
> Far more than we have lost is left us yet.
> —We have enough—I wish indeed that I
> Were younger;—but this hope is a good hope.
> Make ready Luke's best garments, of the best
> Buy for him more, and let us send him forth
> To-morrow, or the next day, or to-night:
> —If he *could* go, the Boy should go to-night."

There are hints here both of forced optimism and of inchoate despair. The sudden impatience at the end of that speech invites the crude inference that Michael simply wants to get things over with. But more remarkable is the coalescence of this impatience with his wish that he were younger. Conceivably that diffidence in his preparation of the legacy surfaces in his distraction and motivates his vain yearning for more time in which to secure his bequest. Yet, sensing the futility of his desires, the father would impetuously banish his son, his reminder that he has "in Shepherd's phrase . . . one foot in the grave."

One might, of course, rather construe his recommendation that the boy be immediately dispatched as a sign of Michael's confidence, a sign that he has, after all, adequately bound his son to the land, so that the boy can safely go abroad to redeem it. Yet Michael's superlative urgency—before there has even been a reply from the prosperous relative regarding the acceptability of the whole scheme—arouses our suspicion that in this crisis *all* his thoughts have turned unrealistic.

I would suggest, in any case, that the rapid ebb and flow of Michael's response to Luke's departure is genetically akin to that rhetorical vacillation in the induction, where the poet now confidently proffered and now uneasily qualified his own legacy. It was the thought of the legacy itself, given the social- and literary-historical situation in which he extended it, that made for the contradictory moods.

Michael's behavior late in the narrative bespeaks an exactly analogous psychology: in one instance, we learn from Isabel that "all his hopes [are] gone"; in the next, we are struck by his boldness—Luke "shall depart to-morrow." But through all his fluctuations there recurs the shepherd's mental recourse to his lost youth. In his final conversation with Luke, Michael recalls his son's infancy:

> Never to living ear came sweeter sounds
> Than when I heard thee by our own fire-side
> First uttering, without words, a natural tune.

Just as Wordsworth, in his induction, reverts to the hour of "domestic tales . . . / Of Shepherds," to the amusements of the fireside or the summer shade, so here Michael nostalgically recollects a time when Luke was "natural," when his utterances were "without words." It is a detail, yet one that perfectly fits Wordsworth's own nostalgia for the period from infancy to young boyhood. "I cannot," as he says in "Tintern Abbey," "paint [i.e., say] what then I was, when first / I came among these hills." Those were the hours of "thoughtless youth," and Michael wishes his son back into those hours; the child is father of the man, to cite another text, yet the father's relation to the child becomes uncertain as the child moves out of his unspoken naturalism and into an articulable consciousness. Certainly "Michael" is not a mere allegory of poetic history but also a persuasive tale of pathos: the old man's crisis is deepened by the growing independence of his son, who finds the prospect of walking down from "among these hills" exciting.

But although Michael appears magnanimous enough to understand his son's high spirits, he persistently reminds Luke of his raising, of its continuity with the past . . . and with the pastoral:

> Even to the utmost I have been to thee
> A kind and a good father; and herein
> I but repay a gift which I myself
> Received at others' hands; for, though now old
> Beyond the common life of man, I still
> Remember them who loved me in my youth.

Michael's hope is that Luke will be similarly mindful of his parent's country-kindness, and it is a hope the more fervent for the father's concurrent disillusionment at seeing so little profit from sixty years' work:

> "Till I was forty years of age, not more
> Than half of my inheritance was mine.
> I toiled and toiled; God blessed me in my work,
> And till these three weeks past the land was free.
> —It looks as if it never could endure
> Another Master. . . ."

Mastery—if not actually pastoral, at least poetically so—is likewise the issue for Wordsworth. He and his character find themselves forced to cling to it, because it is scarcely clear who may succeed them.

Michael, for example, knows that his son departs into danger. Even as he asks Luke to lay the first stone in the sheep-fold that marks their covenant, he sounds an ominous note:

> ". . . whatever fate
> Befal thee, I shall love thee to the last,
> And bear thy memory with me to the grave."

The comment betrays a proleptic resignation. The memory which he will sustain is the dream of his pastoralism's survival in a second self. But Luke, it seems inevitably, soon begins

To slacken in his duty; and, at length,
He in the dissolute city gave himself
To evil courses; ignominy and shame
Fell on him, so that he was driven at last
To seek a hiding-place beyond the seas.

It is noteworthy that Luke's disgrace is unspecific. There is an echo, though apparently an inverse one, of the experience of Richard Bateman, the parish-boy who left the hills with a basket "filled with pedlar's wares," subsequently also moved "beyond the seas," and ultimately caused the construction in his native place of an elaborate church with a floor of marble, "sent from foreign lands." We dare not over-speculate, yet perhaps Luke's ways are evil in Michael's mind alone—we have, after all, no details about them, only the shepherd's own vivid responses. It may be that the boy's crime is foremost the breach of the pastoral covenant: he has gone metaphorically as well as literally into foreign parts, just as Richard the parish boy has supplanted the simplicity of his rearing-place with the spoils of mercantilism, however disguised.

If that is a tenuous interpretation, no alternative one leaps obviously to mind. Immediately following the vague passage describing Luke's "evil courses," we read that

There is a comfort in the strength of love;
'Twill make a thing endurable, which else
Would overset the brain. . . .

Note however that the old man never himself expresses grief, nor does he invite pity. It is Wordsworth here who steps boldly into the poem for the first time since the induction in order to assert the calmative power of love, its capacity quite literally to stave off mental breakdown.

But to what kind of love does he refer? The context again suggests less love of the boy, which, as we recall, was never instinctive, than love of the land, which, as for Wordsworth, always was. The narrative nears conclusion, but Michael is outwardly unchanged. The poet's final description of him recalls, part of it *verbatim,* the initial one, and once more it could serve as self-portrait:

Among the rocks
He went, and still looked up to sun and cloud,
And listened to the wind; and, as before,

Performed all kinds of labor for his sheep,
And for the land, his small inheritance.

The old man's strength abides in his commitment to "sheepland," yet that strength now serves time and not a future ideal, a fact that lends more, not less pathos to the line that Matthew Arnold took to be exemplarily Wordsworthian: "And never lifted up a single stone."

Throughout his poetry, Wordsworth confronts his own fear of potential loss—a fear that the Muse will falter, that the poet will leave his mission unachieved or, what is the same thing, insufficiently powerful to live on in the minds of later natural hearts. Likewise for Michael: although Luke violates the covenant with his father, the father defaults on the contract, too, "and left the work unfinished when he died." In the end, for all his impassioned pastoralism, the old man's land does pass into a stranger's hand, and that stranger's concerns are economic, not pastoral at all:

> The cottage which was named THE EVENING STAR
> Is gone—the ploughshare has been through the ground
> On which it stood; great changes have been wrought
> In all the neighbourhood: yet the oak is left
> That grew beside their door; and the remains
> Of the unfinished Sheep-fold may be seen
> Beside the boisterous brook of Greenhead Ghyll.

One emblem of pastoralism remains in THE CLIPPING TREE, but there is none to comprehend its significance; it can no longer take dominion, and is now a ritual reference devoid of its referent.

But in fact how tenuous this ritualistic pastoralism has been from the start! Michael had depended on "one inmate," who betrayed him; he had performed his ministry under the oak tree, which "stood single," and lived in a cottage which likewise "stood single," commanding the prospect but precarious and vulnerable in its isolation. How *very* blind the old man's "blind love" for his flock and pastures now seems to have been. Wordsworth surely has reasons to share his hero's anguish, his literary situation the mythical analogue to the shepherd's literal one.

This dark note is the clearer if we compare "Michael" to a "Pastoral Song" from the preceding poetical epoch. Let us use one familiar to Wordsworth,[4] William Collins's "Ode to Evening," which has its probable source in "conventional odes to an evening star"; for *"To the Evening Star* was a well-known 'idyllium' attributed to Moschus [and] . . . often translated in the eighteenth century,"[5] a kind of Ur-pastoral.

If Collins had a poetical goal quintessentially akin to Wordsworth's—namely, the discovery of a poetic mode and matter congenial to Enlightened Britain—still the diction of his "pastoral" ("now the bright-hair'd Sun / Sits in yon western Tent") displays the protracted influence, odious to Wordsworth, of neoclassic refinement; and Collins's resolution in the hailing of polite graces *("Fancy, Friendship, Science,* smiling *Peace")* actually contravenes Wordsworth's deepest impulses. Clearly, by his standards, the "Ode to Evening" would be pastoral only in the most attenuated sense. His own poem vigorously banishes the diluting artificialities of sensibility.

Yet Collins can at least claim that it is the rising of Hesperus which prompts his song. For him the star of evening is still the "folding star," the signal for herdsmen to send their sheep to fold. At the end of "Michael," neither the pastors nor the sheep survive, even in a gilded literary form. Indeed the EVENING STAR itself—Michael's cottage—has vanished almost out of memory, and the fold, unfinished, is but "a straggling heap of unhewn stones!"

We are deliberately sent back to the induction, with all its hopes and doubts, by the final distych of the poem, and the reversion weights our reading, makes "Michael" an even more chastening document than readers have commonly supposed. In retrospect we discover a novel reason why the landmark that Wordsworth singles out so held his imagination. In the old shepherd's fate, and particularly in his relation to his son—a relation expressed by that ruined sheepfold—the poet found a living emblem for his historical position in poetry and for what he may uneasily have construed as a potentially intestate death.

In spite of his passionate proprietorship of the pastoral vision associated with hills and fields, Wordsworth in "Michael" may have felt that his was the last such proprietorship. The actual evening star sets soon after rising, and it is part of Wordsworth's self-understanding here that his poetry initiates a mode perhaps doomed to disappear shortly after its ascent. What could be more debilitating to the greatest of memory-poets than the thought that he alone had a memory.

NOTES

1. Stephen M. Parrish, *The Art of the Lyrical Ballads* (Cambridge: Harvard University Press, 1973), 187.

2. Parrish, *Art of the Lyrical Ballads,* 162.

3. Geoffrey Hartman, *Wordsworth's Poetry, 1798–1814* (New Haven: Yale University Press, 1964), 262.

4. See notes to "An Evening Walk" in *The Poetical Works of William Wordsworth,*

ed. E. de Selincourt, vol. I (Oxford: Oxford Press, 1940), ed. E. de Selincourt, 318–29 *passim*.

5. Geoffrey Hartman, "Romantic Poetry and the Genius Loci," in *Beyond Formalism* (New Haven: Yale University Press, 1970), 322, 322n. In such recent essays as "Evening Star and Evening Land" (*The Fate of Reading* [Chicago: University of Chicago Press, 1975]), Hartman develops a notion that colors my argument and my reading of English (and later American) poetry in general: that poets since Milton have sought a "Hesperean" muse to express national character through a new kind of nature-poetry.

From Sublime to Rigamarole

Relations of Frost to Wordsworth

⚭

I. Heirs and Heirlessness

GIVEN THEIR MUTUAL ATTRACTION to nature, pastoral, and ballad, it is unsurprising that Robert Frost saw in Wordsworth a primary influence.[1] His famous claim that *North of Boston* "dropped to an everyday level of diction that even Wordsworth kept above" shows that influence;[2] it also shows the competitive stance that Frost always adopted toward this ancestor. Consider the turns of a lengthy speech, the "Tribute to Wordsworth" given at Cornell University's 1950 symposium commemorating the centennial of Wordsworth's death. Frost starts by noticing the brevity of Wordsworth's major period, but quickly protests, "I'm not here to take away from him at all."[3] Yet he persistently deflects attention from Wordsworth, either by digression (protracted quotations from other poets) or by diffusing Wordsworth's prominence in the occasion, let alone in poetic tradition: "People ask me what I read. Why, I read Shakespeare, and I read Wordsworth, and I read almost anything." The process of refocusing is generally ironic or left-handed: "But I haven't by dislike or distaste eliminated much of Wordsworth. Most of it will do very well."

The speech thus establishes a triple affective structure: distraction from Wordsworth, doubt about his accomplishment (his "tone . . . of Simple Simon," his "insipidity," his "banal" quality), and final, partial qualification of doubt:

I think that's the essential Wordsworth. That lovely banality and that penetration that goes with it. It goes right down into the soul of man, and always, there'll be one line that's just as penetrating as anything anybody ever wrote.

Of course, the ordering of components in that structure is variable:

Let's say one of Wordsworth's. (I don't want to act as if the only poet I didn't know was Wordsworth, after I've come here to celebrate him.) You know what I'd read you if I could? I'd read

"Michael." That I've always admired very, very much, but it's too long, and as I looked at it this afternoon . . . I found it went on page after page. I'd forgotten that. It had made a better impression on me than that.

What, then, was the influence Frost felt? Simply, not a so-called Romantic one; indeed, Frost comes closest to direct tribute in remarks on "Ode to Duty," in which Wordsworth discards his own "Romanticism." It is this disenchanted poet who informs Frost's work, but Frost, with real acuteness, had heard the disenchanted voice even in the assured poetry of Wordsworth's egotistical sublime. In this essay I will try to read Wordsworth's poems as Frost did, for Frost's canon may be seen as a purgation of Wordsworth's, "dropping" below his predecessor's in more than stylistic ways, dispelling even the vestigial illusions, as Frost views them, of the chastened Wordsworth. As we shall see, it displaces Imagination with *Fancy* (or "Yankee" skepticism: unwillingness to suspend disbelief, wit, or reason). Pastoral retreat concomitantly collapses into stingy timbered-land, belief in a possible sublime into stubborn earthiness, poem as redemption into poem as "rigamarole."

If Frost scoured his ancestor's legacy, the gesture might have hurt Wordsworth but probably not have surprised him. Though, like any artist, Wordsworth was much concerned with the very matter of legacy, major poems of the Great Decade suggest something more like obsession.[4] In "Lines Composed a Few Miles Above Tintern Abbey," for example, the writer revisits a place connected with "the soul / Of all [his] moral being" in order to assure himself "That in this moment there is life and food / For future years"; but it is his sister who signals hope even beyond those years, for she will recall her brother's "exhortations," the climactic turns of the poem itself, and provide him with at least a serial immortality.

Yet a kind of undertone throughout the poem bespeaks the writer's worry lest his reader assume a Frostian skepticism toward its assertions. Here, the word "exhortations" betrays unease behind Wordsworth's "cheerful faith" in imaginative legacy. We read in it an inkling of the self-subduing gestures of reaction, later poems like "Ode to Duty" or "Elegiac Stanzas" that at once validate the unease and seek support in acceptance and endurance.

Beginning with his forefather's belatedly acquired clarity, Frost proceeded often to witticize it. Indeed, we can ourselves fancifully construe certain Frost lyrics as disenchantedly Wordsworthian, as ironic "replies"[5] to pieces like "Tintern Abbey" which open onto faith in posterity:

Much as I own I owe
The passers of the past
Because their to and fro
Has cut this road to last,
I owe them more today
Because they've gone away

And come not back with steed
And chariot to chide
My slowness with their speed
And scare me to one side.
They have found other scenes
For haste and other means.

They leave the road to me
To walk in saying naught
Perhaps but to a tree
Inaudibly in thought,
"From you the road receives
A priming coat of leaves.

"And soon for lack of sun
The prospects are in white
It shall be further done,
But with a coat so light
The shape of leaves will show
Beneath the brush of snow."

And so on into winter
Till even I have ceased
To come as a foot printer,
And only some slight beast
So mousy or so foxy
Shall print there as my proxy.[6]

The first four lines want only end-stopping to be a complete, alternately rhymed quatrain; we read them so in passing, and momentarily suppose a confession of total debt: the poet "owes" all he "owns" to pioneers. But the end of the stanza corrects the misreading its introduction invites. Frost's gratitude is that they have "gone away" and left for him a clearing. ("Closed for Good," aptly, would at last appear in *In the Clearing*.) Given the "steeds" and "chariots" in the next stanza, we must strain to assume that Frost refers only to departed farmers; yet we needn't choose, for the poem merges literal and literary path-breakers (note the play on "leaves" and "prints" throughout). Frost here turns *all* his predecessors into epic figures. But this merely prepares us for further irony, for disenchanted commentary as in "Tintern Abbey": "They have found other scenes / For haste and other means." Like the poem at large, these amount to vacancy and silence. Frost dismisses the premise of Wordsworth's "cheerful faith," that some generous and perpetual force linking mind and nature survives in a poem's accomplishment.

It's just that the world Frost enters is miserly: earlier passers have bequeathed him only this slight road "To walk in saying naught." The quoted but inaudible address to a tree, then, in stanzas 3 and 4 constitutes mute poem within poem (like Wordsworth's address to his sister), but sets terms of natural perception contradictory to those of "Tintern Abbey." "From you," says Frost, "the road receives / A priming coat of leaves." With nature's priming gesture, Wordsworth blends his own gesture; for unlike Frost's exclusively visual and silent world, Wordsworth's scene involves the "eye and ear,—both what they half create / And what perceive." While "the light of setting suns" was for Wordsworth part of a sober but sustaining "motion and a spirit, that impels / All thinking things, all objects of all thought," Frost finds a grimmer impulse in nature:

> "And soon for lack of sun
> The prospects are in white
> It shall be further done,
> But with a coat so light
> The shape of leaves will show
> Beneath the brush of snow."

The inner Frost poem is also a poem of inner frost. Autumnal, conscious of its transitoriness, it does not blend with, but reflects the gathering cold of its natural scene. Yet even the reflection is but half successful, for the poet's "leaves" are like nature's only in falling, not in the prospect of return. The final stanza, a meditation on the interstitial lyric, shows that nature, however gradually, impels the assays of this "foot printer" (a canny trope for metrically fastidious poet) back to the status of the blank page. Even if we ignore Frost's pun on heirlessness ("lack of sun"), the tough wit of his ending implies his poetic fate: winter will erase his "prints" and "only some slight beast . . . / Shall print there as [his] proxy." Frost substitutes stark declaration for exhortation, lacking the consolation of human continuity embodied in Wordsworth's Dorothy.

The degeneracy of Frost's actual (and un-Wordsworthian) context—the clearings reverted to second-growth woods and puckerbrush—drives home the lessons of "Closed for Good." One of his letters appropriately suggested this flinty lyric as "a new end piece symbolically" for the 1949 reissue of *North of Boston*. We know that volume's announcement of competition with Wordsworth, so that if there is self-irony in the letter when Frost pledges also "to write a small preface to go desperately down to posterity with," there may too be wry reference to the last great writer of prefaces (*Letters*, 178–79).

And of "desperate" ones, if we adopt a Frostian view: consider the 1800 preface to *Lyrical Ballads*, which seeks among other things to justify the use of country language as "a more permanent, and a far more philosophical" mode than that of the contemporary polite world, or of passers past. Even idealizing Frost's "pastoral" agenda, we cannot imagine him speaking so. Yet Wordsworth's very style, apologetic and circumlocutory, suggests that Wordsworth was hard put to overcome Frostian skepticism not only in his readers but also perhaps in himself. It is not, for example, he who is anxious to defend the permanent relevance of his language or his material:

> Several of my Friends are anxious for the success of these Poems, from a belief, that, if the views with which they were composed were indeed realised, a class of Poetry would be produced, well adapted to interest mankind permanently, and not unimportant in the quality, and in the multiplicity of its moral relations.

Wordsworth does not claim personal success. But if someone were to achieve his aims, pleasure "would be produced"; this is not to say obviously significant pleasures, but "not unimportant" ones. And so on. Wordsworth's claim is for the potential and not the actual value of his volume, its status as the model of a model. Because it *promises* so much, friends "have advised me to prefix a systematic defense of the theory upon which the Poems were written":

> But I was unwilling to undertake the task, knowing that on the occasion, the Reader would look coldly upon my arguments, since I might be suspected of having been principally influenced by the selfish and foolish hope of *reasoning* him into an approbation of these particular Poems.

Does Wordsworth's diffidence about the particular poems arise from fear that their prospects will ultimately be closed for good? Such an assumption would lead to even soberer revision of "Tintern Abbey," which often suggests a cognate indirection:

> If this
> Be but a vain belief, yet oh! how oft
> In darkness and amid the many shapes
> Of joyless daylight; when the fretful stir
> Unprofitable, and the fever of the world,
> Have hung upon the beatings of my heart
> How oft, in spirit, have I turned to thee!
> O sylvan Wye, thou wanderer thro' the woods,
> How often has my spirit turned to thee!
>
> (ll. 49–57)[7]

Turnings and returnings of the mind—repetitive, often—counter the momentary fear of vanity. Yet Frost, whose sense of the world implies debilitatingly abrupt progression without return, would construe such palliative wandering as self-delusion or masked apology.

The passage just quoted follows the famous one "in which the burthen of the mystery, / In which the heavy and the weary weight / Of all this unintelligible world / Is lightened" and, "almost suspended," "we see into the life of things." The blankness of "Closed for Good" represents Frost's general wariness of such lightening and penetration. Even in "Birches," where a dual mental movement, back in time and upward from life's "burthen," seems at one point to recall "Tintern Abbey," Frost's unwillingness to rise through imagination to "Intellectual Love" (*Prelude*, IV.207) reveals itself in the end:

> So was I once myself a swinger of birches,
> And so I dream of going back to be.
> It's when I'm weary of considerations,
> And life is too much like a pathless wood
> Where your face tickles and bums with the cobwebs
> Broken across it, and one eye is weeping
> From a twig's having lashed across it open,
> I'd like to get away from earth awhile. . . .

Yet Frost abruptly checks his dream of being "almost suspended":

> And then come back to it and begin over.
> May no fate willfully misunderstand me
> And half grant what I wish and snatch me away

> Not to return. Earth's the right place for love:
> I don't know where it's likely to go better.

The "weariness" comes, in this beautiful passage and the one it echoes, from life in the fragmented adult world. Frost refrains here from urbanizing this malaise, yet the yearning in either poem is a pastoral one for uncluttered zones beyond confusion. "The world is too much with us," says a Wordsworth sonnet that adumbrates a pastoral remedy as does Frost's "New Hampshire": "Me for the hills where I don't have to choose." For both poets the northern return is a regression to simplified decisions and values.[8]

However, the simplification does not console Frost the way Wordsworth claims it does him, as another juxtaposition—"Lines Written in Early Spring" and Frost's "Spring Pools"—will attest. The former stresses a blending intrinsic to the natural scene:

> I heard a thousand blended notes,
> While in a grove I sate reclined,
> In that sweet mood when pleasant thoughts
> Bring sad thoughts to the mind.
>
> To her fair works did Nature link
> The human soul that through me ran;
> And much it grieved my heart to think
> What man has made of man.
>
> Through primrose tufts, in that green bower,
> The periwinkle trailed its wreaths;
> And 'tis my faith that every flower
> Enjoys the air it breathes.
>
> The birds around me hopped and played,
> Their thoughts I cannot measure,
> But the least motion that they made,
> It seemed a thrill of pleasure.
>
> The budding twigs spread out their fan,
> To catch the breezy air;
> And I must think, do all I can,
> That there was pleasure there.
>
> If this belief from Heaven be sent,
> If such be Nature's holy plan,
> Have I not reason to lament
> What man has made of man?

The lyric implies the conviction, elaborately voiced in longer poems, that nature as well as man delights in harmony, yet shows that the conviction can never empirically be validated. Hence, the illogical leaps in all the poem's stanzas: the periwinkles bloom, "and *'tis my faith* that every flower / Enjoys the air it breathes"; the musical birds have thoughts immeasurable, and their sporting "*seemed* a thrill of pleasure." Or, most odd, the twigs catch the breeze, "And I must think, *do all I can,* / That there was pleasure there." That first line, apparently a groping for rhyme, is actually a protest of faith against the fear that natural reciprocity may only be a fancy, or what is the same, only seemingly a signal of pleasure. The fear is, if at all, only partly overcome in the ballad, which ends quite conditionally: "If this belief from Heaven be sent, / If such be Nature's holy plan." Wordsworth would have his belief in pleasure through reciprocity attain the status of imaginative myth, but cannot here assert that status.

He has at the outset described himself, illogically, as being in that "sweet mood" that causes sadness: the very business of feeling so good raises the specter of opposite feeling, pleasure in harmony the specter of disharmony, and vernal vision the specter of winter. He laments "what man has made of man," which is, of course, pastoral reaction against industrialism and the mentality spawned by it, but also against "man" as adult, victim/perpetrator of complexity and fragmentation as opposed to the fullness and simplicity of seedtime. Wordsworth's pastoral tendency is always linked with nature (whose objects themselves persistently interfuse); if the adult poet cannot link the human soul to natural pleasure, he will have no pastoral—or will be grimly aware of the past in "pastoral," the fallacy in what we once called pathetic fallacy. Written as a companion piece to "To My Sister," moreover, "Early Spring" is part of the legacy that Wordsworth extends to us through his exhortations to Dorothy: a legacy, he knows, of disenchantment if indeed his faith proves no more than a fancy.

In spite of his lyric's anguish and lamentation, though, Wordsworth at least hopes for a possible association of natural and human renewals, unlike Frost in his spring meditation:

SPRING POOLS

These pools that, though in forest, still reflect
The total sky almost without defect,
And like the flowers beside them, chill and shiver,
Will like the flowers beside them soon be gone,
And yet not out by any brook or river,
But up by roots to bring dark foliage on.

The trees that have it in their pent up buds
To darken nature and be summer woods—
Let them think twice before they use their powers
To blot out and drink up and sweep away
These flowery waters and these watery flowers
From snow that melted only yesterday.

Frost's poem also invites a view of natural harmony, if only the most tenuous kind (note the subordination of the opening stanza, which qualifies that harmony as it announces it); yet its speaker—far less active than Wordsworth's—does not project the connection of landscape and sky beyond the moment. Indeed, he has no power to do so, for all agency is nature's: nature appears to be "souled" (may even "think twice"), but is also latently violent (note the "pent up buds" like caged beasts). Immediately as she brightens, teasing us with synthesis "almost without defect," she darkens, and this is partly because of *contest* among the objects of nature.

Wordsworth, perhaps feeling the chill of such bleak progression and strife, still does "all he can" to contravene it, so that the threat of disharmony in the scene occurs to us only as inference from his over-protest. Nothing rises up from Frost's landscape to motivate such compensatory effort. The poet eschews lament, because he sees the absoluteness of change and degeneration, the futility of complaint.

Of course the pools themselves rise up, "But up by roots to bring dark foliage on." This is not the upward movement of Wordsworth's poem (grove-flowers-birds-trees-air and finally "Heaven"), which suggests sublimation, but an upwardness to obliteration: the quick future will "blot out and drink up and sweep away" the scene that merges flower, water, and sky.

Wordsworth, simply, fears vacancy; Frost assumes it, because instants of natural fullness are so fleeting as to be delusory, and human achievement is almost equally so. The Frost of "Spring Pools" remains an observer rather than a rhetorician because, as his scene persuades him, it is feckless to exhort the void. One needs an heir to supply a legacy: poetic stasis (as in "Closed for Good") is, like natural stasis, momentary.

Consider poems in which Frost imagines *himself* as the heir to an artist; his befuddlement in that role shows how foreign are an artifact's genesis and context to its observers, how insufficient therefore art as monument. The stonecutter of "To an Ancient," for example, has "two claims to immortality": "You made the eolith, you grew the bone." Rather than consolation *(ars longa, vita brevis)*, Frost oddly offers the second—the bone—as "more peculiarly your own, / And likely to have been enough alone." Enough for what? For immortality? Surely not: even bodily traces outlast man's making, such that Wordsworth's faith is in danger of ceding to despair. The interrogatives of Frost's final stanza may moot the despair, but do not cancel its threat:

> You make me ask if I would go to time
> Would I gain anything by using rhyme?
> Or aren't the bones enough to lime?

Frost says in "A Missive Missile" (as so often, he puns, and doubly stresses *missing*) that "Someone in ancient Mas d'Azil / Took a little pebble wheel / And dotted it with red for me, / And sent it to me years and years."
He then fancies that

> . . . his ghost is standing by
> Importunate to give the hint
> And be successfully conveyed.
> How anyone can fail to see
> Where perfectly in form and tint
> The metaphor, the symbol lies!
> Why will I not analogize?
> (I do too much in some men's eyes.)
> O slow, uncomprehending me,
> Enough to make a spirit moan
> Or rustle in a bush or tree.
> I have the ocher written flint,
> The two dots and the ripple line.
> The meaning of it is unknown,
> Or else I fear entirely mine. . . .

Frost himself, of course, suffers several ironies here. A poet's skepticism of art is necessarily self-skepticism, and the poem's jogging tetrameter may itself suggest inconsequence. Moreover, the poet, if anything overly given to metaphor and analogy, misses the meaning of this missile sent over time; who then will grasp it? The stone seems to ask Frost for an analogy between primitive and modern makers, perhaps as deathless figures, but he represses this response, which would signal the sublimely egotistical postulation of "the noble living and the noble dead" (*Prelude*, XI.395). Frost's chiding of himself, like that of "Closed for Good," for slowness and incomprehension is misleading, for he knows that any "comprehension" would be self-fabricated. As Wordsworth, in temporary disillusionment about the lives and legacies of earlier poets, said: "By our own spirits are we deified." Compare Frost's equally double-edged line: "The metaphor, the symbol lies!" Distortion and self-deception are inevitable, for

> Far as we aim our signs to reach,
> Far as we often make them reach,
> Across the soul-from-soul abyss,
> There is an aeon-limit set
> Beyond which souls are doomed to miss.
> Two souls may be too widely met.
> That sad-with-distance river beach
> With mortal longing may beseech;
> It cannot speak as far as this.

Frost, of course, implies that the artifact's obscurity is a product of its antiquity; but this is to quibble. The process whereby soul and soul lapse into incommunication may indeed be long, but is inevitable. If the message wrought in stone is cloudy, then what, our inveterate punster might ask, are words worth?

II. From Pastoral Sublime to Rigamarole

Still we must deal with equivalently playful yet far tenderer work like "Directive," a poem that actually accepts a legacy and proffers one, thereby pointedly recalling Wordsworth's "Michael." Like so many of Wordsworth's poems, "Michael" is motivated by the search for landscape to serve "as a kind of permanent rallying point for [the] domestic feelings . . . as a tablet upon which they are written which makes them objects of memory in a thousand instances when they should otherwise be forgotten."[9]

The livelihood of Wordsworth's shepherd thus has a kind of immemorial quality. His cottage, for example, is dignified by being called THE EVENING STAR, as if constellated in some mythic order, which the curious *ritualism* of this poem in fact implies:

> . . . in a later time, ere yet the Boy
> Had put on man's attire, did Michael love,
> Albeit of a stem, unbending mind,
> To have the Young-one in his sight, when he

Wrought in the field, or on his shepherd's stool
Sate with a fettered sheep before him stretched
Under the large old oak, that near his door
Stood single, and, from matchless depth of shade,
Chosen for the Shearer's covert from the sun,
Thence in our rustic dialect was called
THE CLIPPING TREE, a name which yet it bears.
There, while they two were sitting in the shade,
With others round them, earnest all and blithe,
Would Michael exercise his heart with looks
Of fond correction and reproof bestowed
Upon the child, if he disturbed the sheep. . . .

(ll. 159–74)

In spite of fondness, Michael will not countenance disruption of this literal pastoral mode: "correction" of the boy is essential to his initiation into that mode, whose sacredness is betokened, for example, by the shrine-like CLIPPING TREE.

The pathos of "Michael" lies above all in the dissolution of ritualized land and relation to land: ultimately THE EVENING STAR is gone, and THE CLIPPING TREE remains as anomaly in a transformed countryside. The search for permanence reveals itself as illusion, save that Wordsworth claims to have turned his very narrative into testimony to timeless pastoral values. The poet accepts the legacy that the son has refused and that acceptance proves a saving grace against the degenerative drive of history.[10]

Defending "Directive" against the interpretation that insists on its clear and disenchanted perception, David Sanders sees a Wordsworthian gesture on Frost's part: the poet turns "make-believe ritual into ritual make-believe that carries the poem to its denouement." But Frost's "ritual make-believe" is precisely *founded* on disenchanted clarity of view. Not to see this is to idealize; for example:

> The handing down of the vessel to the children, to the poet, and finally to us, suggests how life renews itself imaginatively as it does so physically. . . . As our salvation depends on him, so his survival depends on us. If the poem is necessary for him to save us, we are necessary if the poem shall save him.[11]

This reading attributes a positive stance toward imaginative legacy to one deeply skeptical on that issue; its moral applies more obviously to the source poem, "Michael," which does unironically offer a salvational scheme: Wordsworth hopes to excite

> Profitable sympathies in many kind and good hearts, and . . . in some small degree enlarge our feelings of reverence for our species, and our knowledge of human nature. . . . I thought, at a time when these feelings are sapped in so many ways, that ["Michael" and "The Brothers"] might cooperate, however feebly.[12]

But in "Directive," according to its author, "The poet is not offering any general salvation. . . . In the midst of this now too much for us he tells everyone to go back . . . to whatever source they have" (Thompson, *Robert Frost*, 3: 136).

Salvation depends not on the poet but on ourselves: it is, moreover, a provisional fiction that tomorrow will undo. Frost sees as much in the landscape. It took literally centuries for the English north country to reach the pass lamented in "Michael"—

> The cottage which was named THE EVENING STAR,
> Is gone—the ploughshare has been through the ground
> On which it stood; great changes have been wrought
> In all the neighbourhood: yet the oak is left
> That grew beside their door; and the remains
> Of the unfinished Sheepfold may be seen
> Beside the boisterous brook of Greenhead Ghyll . . .
>   (ll. 476–82)

But north of Boston, beside the waters of "Directive," this process has been effected in less than a hundred years: the shepherds built their stone fences, and were destroyed by the Australian and Southwestern mutton industry; next, the dirt farmers passed their ploughshares through the ground, exposing the granite ribs that forced them off it; then the timber barons cut down the pine and oak:

> As for the woods' excitement over you
> That sends light rustle rushes to their leaves,
> Charge that to upstart inexperience.
> Where were they all not twenty years ago?

The pastoral clearings have gone back to scrub growth and the whips of steeple bush that give the volume in which "Directive" appears its name. The leavings of pastors past do not make for lasting vision:

> Back in a time made simple by the loss
> Of detail, burned, dissolved, and broken off
> Like graveyard marble sculpture in the weather,
> There is a house that is no more a house
> Upon a farm that is no more a farm
> And in a town that is no more a town.
> The road there, if you'll let a guide direct you
> Who only has at heart your getting lost,
> May seem as if it should have been a quarry—
> Great monolithic knees the former town
> Long since gave up pretense of keeping covered.
> And there's a story in a book about it:
> Besides the wear of iron wagon wheels
> The ledges show lines ruled southeast northwest,
> The chisel work of an enormous glacier
> That braced his feet against the Arctic Pole. . . .

Both Wordsworth and Frost guide us up an uncouth road and back to a story, urging us to lose our complicated selves and to find truer ones. But there is a characteristically mischievous ring in Frost's invitation, as if the retreat in time freed us for whimsy rather than for Wordsworthian moral vigor. Frost's "tale" never gets beyond the deliberately vague and playful hints of his opening lines, while Wordsworth reconstructs a long and serious story:

> It was the first
> Of those domestic tales that spake to me
> Of Shepherds, dwellers in the valleys, men
> Whom I already loved. . . .
> And hence this Tale, while I was yet a Boy
> Careless of books, yet having felt the power
> Of Nature, by the gentle agency
> Of natural objects, led me on to feel
> For passions that were not my own, and think
> (At random and imperfectly indeed)
> On man, the heart of man, and human life.
>
> (ll. 21–33)

Much has to do with the poets' divergent views of nature. Frost stresses the bluntness of her "simplifying" (note the brute monosyllables, the harsh descriptives, the chill in the passage just cited). She is both gentle agent and inspiration to Wordsworth, and having felt her influence as both, Wordsworth confidently assumes a similar effect on his characters, especially Michael:

> Those fields, those hills—what could they less? had laid
> Strong hold on his affections, were to him
> A pleasurable feeling of blind love,
> The pleasure that there is in life itself. . . .
>
> (ll. 74–77)

Frost, eyes wide open, climbs his road as a stranger to such pastoralism (if ever it existed), skeptical of all stories—"in a book" or not—concerning it. "Directive" remains inchoate narrative, because the poet has not invented as he urges us to do:

> Make yourself up some cheering song of how
> Someone's road home from work this once was,
> Who may be just ahead of you on foot
> Or creaking with a buggy load of grain.
> The height of the adventure is the height
> Of country where two village cultures faded
> Into each other. Both of them are lost.
> And if you're lost enough to find yourself
> By now, pull in your ladder road behind you
> And put a sign up CLOSED to all but me.
> Then make yourself at home.
> The only field now left's no bigger than a harness gall.
> First there's the children's house of make-believe,
> Some shattered dishes underneath a pine,
> The playthings in the playhouse of the children.
> Weep for what little things could make them glad.

Here is an instance of the peculiar Frostian tenderness that Wordsworth could never have managed, partly because he sought the broad vision and partly because his country folk, though threatened, still lived; they had not suffered a "loss of detail," for they had not in his view ever attained to complexity. Frost's emphasis on fading and indistinctness signals not interfusion (nor the blindness of love) but ruin brought on by mean climate and pinched nature. Archaic cultures have so melted into one another that the poet coaxes us to spin a make-believe story (an ellipsis for *fanciful history*). He invites us—half jocularly, half wistfully—to indulge our powers of feigning: in the words of

Wordsworth's collaborator on *Lyrical Ballads,* as they appear by happy accident in "Frost at Midnight," to "make a Toy of Thought."

It is worth lingering momentarily with Coleridge, especially his recollection of Wordsworth's role in the 1798 volume:

> Subjects were to be chosen from ordinary life; the characters and incidents were to be such, as will be found in every village and its vicinity, where there is a meditative and feeling mind to seek after them, or to notice them, when they present themselves. . . .

> Mr. Wordsworth . . . was to propose to himself as his object, to give the charm of novelty to things of every day, and to excite a feeling analogous to the supernatural, by awakening the mind's attention from the lethargy of custom, and directing it to the loveliness and the wonders of the world before us.[13]

Coleridge's language reminds us of the eighteenth- and nineteenth-century controversy over sublime and beautiful, and limns his friend's relation to that controversy. Wordsworth's Imagination ("meditative and feeling mind") will *conflate* beautiful ("loveliness") and sublime ("wonders"). Indeed, Wordsworth will defamiliarize the landscape by imbuing the commonplaces of low and rustic life with an awesomeness heretofore reserved for epic or romance. Hence in "Michael," despite its "low" occasion, Wordsworth is unself-conscious about ritualism and straightforward in echoing Scripture, because he feels his naturalist program can arouse sensations akin to the supernatural. In "Directive," ritual has degenerated into whimsical charade, the Scriptural allusions at the end are deliberately near-facetious, the Grail of romance is a shattered plaything, and other romance and supernatural elements—the "eye pairs out of forty firkins," for example—are dismissed as upstarts. There are no characters or incidents besides the nameless ones that Frost fancifully calls up, a fact that shows the priority of his will in making the poem. Wordsworth, as Coleridge notes, is indifferent about priority: in his abundant world, the mind can either "seek after" fit matter for his song, or merely "notice" it, like mild revelation.

However arrived at, the loftiness of Wordsworth's concerns accounts for the urgency of his narrative, which seeks to purge our lethargy and to reveal in pastoral life a holy energy. Consider the title character:

> . . . in his shepherd's calling he was prompt
> And watchful more than ordinary men.

> Hence had he learned the meaning of all winds,
> Of blasts of every tone; and oftentimes,
> When others heeded not, he heard the South
> Make subterraneous music. . . .
> . . . .
>   . . . the storm, that drives
> The traveller to a shelter, summoned him
> Up to the mountains: he had been alone
> Amid the heart of many thousand mists,
> That came to him, and left him, on the heights.
>   (ll. 46–60)

Michael's calling is to elevation and revelation. Coleridge's sense of Wordsworth shows its accuracy as this lowly figure, surrounded by the stormy wind and underworldly music, visits and is visited on the heights, in short as he participates in the very sublime whose language the poet uses here and in such famous passages as *The Prelude* VI and XIV. A rising mountain mist blurs or extinguishes mere sight,[14] and we await a manifestation of the invisible world. Yet, as Coleridge observed, we cannot finally leave things of every day: vision remains nascent, "something ever more about to be," or, in the words of the late Thomas Weiskel:

> In the egotistical sublime the two . . . poles of sensible nature and
> eschatological destination collapse inward and become "habitual"
> attributes of . . . Imagination—a totalizing consciousness whose
> medium is sense but whose power is transcendent. Apocalypse
> becomes immanent; the sublime, a daily habit.[15]

This habitual sublime is part of Wordsworth's crusade against loss and discontinuity, dissipating separations of numinous and actual, generous childhood and ironic adulthood, rendering phenomenological categories of high and low less stark, showing the distinction between "loveliness" and "wonder" no longer to be distinctive.

The effects of such revised sublimity are seen, for example, in Wordsworth's language, which commandeers for common speech the rhetorical energy of the sublime, purging its turgid archaisms but retaining a "height" appropriate to the lofty region that attracts the poet and to his exalted mission for pastoral.

Frost's subsequent purgation of Wordsworth is impelled by the most elementary differences in worldview. We have sensed his skepticism of Wordsworthian "blending"; as he says in a speech on Emerson, the great native Romantic, "a melancholy dualism is the only sound-ness."[16] Frost must inevitably sunder the fusion of low pastoral and sublime *hypsos:* "The height of the adventure is the height / Of country where two village cultures faded." They faded as a star will fade from morning's heaven: Frost's clear daylight vision *desublimates* his context, whereas Wordsworth can poetically reset an EVENING STAR that has literally vanished.

We have seen that the speakers of "Michael" and "Directive" share guide's roles, but our reading should be guided by differences in tone: Wordsworth's call to "courage! for around that boisterous brook / The mountains have all opened out themselves," as opposed to Frost's ex-hortation to privacy, find your *self* and *close* the road. The broad decla-mation of "Michael" disappears from the later poem. It is, after all, a "boisterous" watershed that Wordsworth traces; Frost's is "too lofty and original to rage"; but this is part of make-believe, for nothing of loftiness is evident in the rest of the poem, which also dramatizes the perils of originality. Frost feigns a power in his necessarily lowered voice and diminished scene that they do not have.

Let us, for a moment, pursue this digression on the waters by a con-sideration of Frost's earlier "Hyla Brook" and Wordsworth's hymn to Imagination in *The Prelude* (VI.592–616), relating them as we did "Closed for Good" and "Tintern Abbey." The passage from *The Prelude* runs a familiar course. Imagination signals itself in mist and rises toward supra-natural destiny; then the passage defines (and refuses) the sepa-rateness of destiny and sense. The soul, elevated by imagination, is re-naturalized,

> Strong in herself and in beatitude
> That hides her, like the mighty flood of Nile
> Poured from his font of Abyssinian clouds
> To fertilize the whole Egyptian plain.
> (ll. 614–16)

Quickened, the soul descends powerfully into landscape, imagination marking this movement as one of possible sublimity, of *creative* power, Wordsworth likely borrowing the ancient association of Abyssinia and Eden. The passage's elision of dualism indeed exemplifies the egotisti-cal sublime by fulfilling the ends of what Wordsworth early called his "high argument": to show the reciprocity of mind and external world, and the "creation (by no lower name / Can it be called) which they with blended might / Accomplish" *(The Recluse,* ll. 822–24).

The very imagery of "Hyla Brook"—which like "Closed for

Good" puns on the act of poetic creation—provides its own commentary on the distance between the waters that Wordsworth and Frost look upon:

> By June our brook's run out of song and speed.
> Sought for much after that it will be found
> Either to have gone groping underground
> (And taken with it all the Hyla breed
> That shouted in the mist a month ago,
> Like ghost of sleigh bells in a ghost of snow)—
> Or flourished and come up as jewelweed,
> Weak foliage that is blown upon and bent,
> Even against the way its waters went.
> Its bed is left a faded paper sheet
> Of dead leaves stuck together by the heat—
> A brook to none but who remember long.
> This as it will be seen is other far
> Than with brooks taken otherwhere in song.
> We love the things we love for what they are.

The underground groping of the brook/poem's song is distant indeed from the subterraneous music that Michael hears from the height of land, and the distance of waters from waters implies that of Frost from Wordsworth's imaginative structure: the sublime falling into nature, from which imagination evokes it into the "permanent" status of the poem's "leaves," which, if they come at all, constitute "weak foliage" for Frost.

The portrait of Michael cited a moment ago incorporates the components of the sublime—height, vapor, singing winds—because these insubstantials soften the edges of perception, keeping it, that is, from the sharp sight at work in "Hyla Brook." Wordsworth's object is to liberate us from the despotic bodily eye, "to make," in the words of a more sympathetic successor, "the visible a little hard to see" (Wallace Stevens, "The Creations of Sound"). Wordsworth's commonplace sublime interfuses sensory and mental and natural; it blends up and down, dark and light.

> . . . Visionary power
> Attends the motions of the viewless winds,
> Embodied in the mystery of words:
> There darkness makes abode, and all the host
> Of shadowy things works endless changes,—there,
> As in a mansion like their proper home,

Even forms and substances are circumfused
By that transparent veil with light divine,
And, through the turnings intricate of verse,
Present themselves as objects recognised,
In flashes, and with glory not their own.

(*Prelude*, V. 595–605)

As the imagination tends to sublimity, the influence of objective reality recedes. In the shadowy dimension here described, so different from the simple historical fading of "Directive," mind takes on its own flight of glory—what Wordsworth elsewhere calls its "visionary gleam"—just as Wordsworth in "Michael" raises his own EVENING STAR: a sublimation into turnings of verse of the literal one, now dimmed and degraded in relative importance.

Against all this, the very particularism of Frost, his tendency in "Directive" and generally to earthward, is the clearer. What I now will urge is how small in him is the capacity for the sublime.[17] He presents a falling, not of starry wonder into landscape, but of word into empty prospects and imagination into tentative fancy, so that in his work there is rarely a feeling truly analogous to the supernatural but rather a playing at it.

What, though, of the final directive of "Directive," "Drink and be whole again beyond confusion"? The phrase inevitably summons Frost's famous "figure a poem makes": "It ends in a clarification—not necessarily a great clarification, such as sects and cults are founded on, but a momentary stay against confusion" (Thompson, *Robert Frost,* 3: 31). Yet I have insisted, despite the idealizers, that such clarification is based on disenchanted perception, on desublimation. There is nothing in this figure but figuration, nothing either in "Directive" beyond the moment: indeed, the return to a source in this work may be a return to seeing object as object, a clearing away of complex affective obstacles to gladness, like the children's, at little things.

If Wordsworth asserted that mind and world could interfuse, that their cooperative accomplishment was so mighty as to merit no lower name than creation, Frost in his run-out landscape offers precisely a lowering of poetic claims in general. Little things remain little, for he has neither means nor intention to make great things of small, in the manner of Wordsworth's so-called "higher minds":

Them the enduring and the transient both
Serve to exalt; they build up greatest things
From least suggestions; ever on the watch,

Willing to work and to be wrought upon,
They need not extraordinary calls
To rouse them; in a world of life they live,
By sensible impressions not enthralled,
But by their quickening impulse made more prompt
To hold fit converse with the spiritual world,
And with the generations of mankind
Spread over time, past, present, and to come. . . .

(Prelude, XIV.100–110)

Yet we misjudge and undervalue Frost's poetry if we see in it Romantic Dejection. Wordsworth may finally be the greater poet, but he occasionally suffers the defects—bathos, diffuseness, verbal equivocation, and intellectual uncertainty—of that greatness. Frost's contraction of scope does more than provide him with capacities for local affection unavailable to Wordsworth: if his modesty also entails its flaws—a witty cuteness, evasiveness, triviality—at its best it does offer clarification, however momentary:

> When in doubt there is always form to go on with. Anyone who has achieved the least form to be sure of it, is lost to the larger excruciations. I think it must stroke faith the right way. The artist, the poet, might be expected to be the most aware of such assurance. But it is really everybody's sanity to live by it. Fortunately, too, no forms are more engrossing than those lesser ones we throw off, like vortex rings of smoke, all our individual enterprise and needing nobody's cooperation; a basket, a letter, a garden, a room, an idea, a picture, a poem. For these we haven't to get a team together to play. (Prose, 106–9)

This offhand listing of "a poem" in such random company would have wounded him who sought "to bind together by passion and knowledge the vast empire of human society" (1800 Preface), but Frost's stance permits him a rhetorical self-assurance that the more ambitious forefather never could attain. In a 1949 lecture fittingly called "Some Obstinacy," Frost stressed:

> The first thing to say is that you've got to start getting up things to say to yourself if you want to hold your own. And the prefirst thing to say is that you've got to have an own to hold. . . .
>   Don't be afraid of the word. Get up a rigamarole. And I'm going to get up and show you some rigamaroles I got up for my own defense, you know, for the defense of my position in the course of the years. (Thompson, Robert Frost, 3: 179–80)

Frost's corrective to Wordsworth claims that the proper motive be-hind the sublimest oratory is self-containment. A poem—rid of its ex-altations, its mists, winds, and gleams—should have a temporary quid-dity sufficient to let us hold our own. The poet's rigamarole will be a form thrust up between too much and us.

This disenchanted (as it were, "de-mistified") perspective has criti-cal value for our reading of Wordsworth. It lends some insight, for ex-ample, into the curious induction to "Michael," so full of self-contra-diction and qualification:

> Beside the brook
> Appears a straggling heap of unhewn stones!
> And to that simple object appertains
> A story—unenriched with strange events,
> Yet not unfit, I deem, for the fireside,
> Or for the summer shade. . . .
> . . . .
> . . . although it be a history
> Homely and rude, I will relate the same
> For the delight of a few natural hearts,
> And, with yet fonder feeling, for the sake
> Of youthful poets, who among these hills
> Will be my second self when I am gone.
>
> (ll. 16–39)

The "simple object" moves Wordsworth to exclamatory vehe-mence, which he automatically undercuts with disclaimer and (in the manner of the Prefaces) a double-negative turn: the tale is "not unfit." Wordsworth struggles against a Frostian sense of indifference in the large world, of the poet's small inheritance and small power to pass it on. He directs this "homely and rude" account to "a *few* natural hearts," to a scattering of successor poets, yet even this self-irony must be seen against the grander one: it is telling and heartbreaking that the induction which transmits legacy prefaces a tale of *failed* legacy. "Michael," throughout, anticipates a theme of "Directive": a poem affords a mo-mentary stay against inevitability. Had Wordsworth concerned himself less with the larger excruciations, he might have seen his narrative as rigamarole, as a means of holding his own.

III. A Distant Star

Sadly, Wordsworth may have seen—or sensed—just how much of "Michael" *was* rigamarole. His urge to reset a star (the evening star, significantly, is the star of classical pastoral) remains part of his quest for sublimity, and the assertive voice of the induction marks his desire that the poem have, as heavenly bodies were once supposed to have, a permanent "influence." Contravening all this is the qualifying, self-effacing voice that emerges whenever a stoical attitude like Frost's toward the matter of legacy or influence intrudes.

No wonder Frost protested at Cornell that "Michael" went on "too long." Wordsworth's very dilemma forced him into protraction: though he confronted general evidence of the futility of trust in posterity, the entire thrust of his cheerful faith had always been premised on the validity of that trust. Hence his endless animadversions.

Wordsworth's strategy is, as it were, *misguided* rigamarole. Frost knew that feigning must be understood as feigning in order, paradoxically, for it to have a helpful value; it cannot be rhetorically whipped into value-as-truth. The stay against confusion must be acknowledged as momentary, the figure a poem makes as figuration and not prophetic writ (we should for example "say" our poetry and not feel a need to declaim it).

We can see why Frost should have admired, more straightforwardly than any Wordsworth poem, the "Ode to Duty," the work in which Wordsworth refers to himself as "made lowly wise." The phrase itself, of course, is borrowed from Raphael's advice to Adam in *Paradise Lost* (VIII), which comes, aptly enough, in response to Adam's inquiry about the stars. "Solicit not thy thoughts with matters hid," the archangel urges, and we may like the later Wordsworth translate the exhortation into an enjoinder against seeking that home in infinitude which, according to *The Prelude*, is the abode of greatness . . . and of sublime poetry. "Ode to Duty," to pun on a modern coinage, shows Wordworth's abandonment of his quest to be a poetic star.

In describing "Ode to Duty" as "one that I've gotten as much out of in the way of wisdom as any,"[18] Frost describes his own derivation of lowly wisdom from a poem that is itself a meditation on derived lowly wisdom, as if a poet's inheritance fell farther and farther from heaven through the generations. Wordsworth seems less diminished by such relentless lapse than Frost, yet his diminutive adaptations of Milton in this ode may signal a reversion to Frostian awareness of the unattainability of super-earthly power and sublime poetic power. Not that Frost is unskeptical enough to identify that power with "the God-head's most benignant grace"; what I emphasize is how he shares a sense of limitation with the Wordsworth of the "Duty" ode, an acknowledgment that modern efforts to draw lofty influence into the human realm and to pass it on poetically result from solipsistic "confidence misplaced."

"Ode to Duty" looks elsewhere for confidence, traces Wordsworth's submission to a new control: "Me this unchartered freedom tires; / I feel the weight of chance desires" (ll. 37–38). The very autonomy of the spontaneous, wandering imagination that once lifted from him "the weary weight" of the world is seen itself as a weight, so that the poet now searches for fixity: "My hopes no more must change their name, I long for a repose that ever is the same" (ll. 39–40).

"Ode to Duty" shows, I think, a cleaving to the more modest of the two impulses that constituted the dialectic of "Michael"; it does so even more forthrightly than the "Intimations" ode, also completed in 1804, which nonetheless admits that "nothing can bring back the hour / Of splendour in the grass, of glory in the flower" (ll. 181–82). The old link between starry sublime ("glory") and simple natural object ("flower") is reserved for less ambitious pieces like "I Wandered Lonely As a Cloud" (1804), whose daffodils do appear "continuous as stars." Splendor, glory, and power are no longer figured as perpetual, natural immanences in Wordsworth's major turnings of verse. In "Ode to Duty," especially, the poet addresses an abstracted influence: he admits his ripeness to assume "humbler functions" than the effort to connect landscape and sky via imagination.

The poet of the *Recluse* fragment of 1798 had contended that no sublime theme

> . . . can breed such fear and awe
> As fall upon us often when we look
> Into our Minds, into the Mind of Man.
> (ll. 79–81)

But in this poem, Duty is the star that falls upon us, the "awful power," the "stern Lawgiver." The renowned Wordsworth is the one attracted to the "silent laws" of the heart (see "To My Sister"), or to faith in the mind's capacity to draw astral energy into ordinary objects. Frost's Wordsworth resuscitates a severely hierarchical cosmology:

> Flowers laugh before thee on their beds
> And fragrance in thy footing treads;
> Thou dost preserve the stars from wrong;
> And the most ancient heavens, through thee, are fresh and strong.

Degrees of power and influence are strictly apportioned and "chartered" here: man is, so to say, higher than the flowers and lower than the stars, each of which in turn occupies a separate realm from the other.

Indeed, the visible stars are inferior ones (preserved by Duty): above them are invisible heavens; then Duty, who herself is thrice removed from ultimate power: "Daughter of the voice of God!" The universe shades off into pure inscrutability beyond its perceptible margin.

The poet addresses Duty because she is all of heavenly influence that he can intuit; she is his figure, his translation into moral imperative, of hidden might. And she is presented as a superior star (she is "a light to guide," "the light of truth," having the capacity to lead us on "a blissful course") merely because such figuration, deeply contingent on our limited vision, is as close as the "language really used by men" can reach toward genuine sublimity. A star, withdrawn from us, and relatively constant to us, is simply a model for integrity. "I think," says Frost, "that's where I'd like to say two or three lines out of that . . . as if they were embossed on the page. As if they were embossed. For instance: 'And happy will our nature be / When love is an unerring light.'"[19]

Frost, however elliptically, approves Wordsworth's message concerning the fixity and remoteness of the source of influence: and he can himself point to benefits in our attendant assumption of lowliness, urging us exactly to "Take Something Like a Star," which,

> Not even stooping from its sphere,
> . . . asks a little of us here.
> It asks of us a certain height,
> So when at times the mob is swayed
> To carry praise or blame too far,
> We may take something like a star
> To stay our minds on and be staid.

If unerring light prompts no sublime flight, merely asking "a little of us," the height that we do reach in our modesty is at least a "*certain height*." Frost's star poem (companion piece to "Closed for Good" in the Afterword of *Collected Poems*, 1949) seeks security in a world that historically and ontologically works toward our diminishment; and there is evidence that Wordsworth, like Frost—movingly conscious of how difficult it is to receive and transmit poetic legacy—took late comfort in such purged aspiration.

NOTES

1. Lawrance Thompson, *Robert Frost: The Early Years* (New York: Holt, Rinehart and Winston, 1966), 662. Subsequent references to Thompson's three-volume biogra-

phy—*The Early Years, The Years of Triumph,* and *The Later Years*—will be cited parenthetically as "Thompson, *Robert Frost.*"

2. *Selected Letters of Robert Frost,* ed. Lawrance Thompson (New York: Holt, Rinehart and Winston, 1964), 83–84. Subsequent references will be cited parenthetically as *Letters.*

3. Robert Frost, "Tribute to Wordsworth," Cornell Library Journal 11 (1970): 77–99. Quotations here are from 78, 91, 80, 86, and 88, respectively.

4. Narratives like "Michael" (see the detailed discussion below) and "The Brothers," for example, poignantly ask: What of a man's character and/or works survive his own disappearance or the disappearance of his native ground? Wordsworth may be said always to seek the reassurance, indeed the "joy," proposed in stanza 9 of the "Intimations" ode, "that *in our embers / Is* something that doth live." Wordsworth's deepest hope is that something primary and perpetual can sustain itself even after the vanishing of specific natural context: with this hope in mind, we can see, for example, that a troubled poem like "Resolution and Independence"—generated by the poet's meditation on "Mighty poets in their misery dead"—and an apparently tranquil one like "I Wandered Lonely as a Cloud" have much in common: the vision of sturdiness and dignity in the leech gatherer, despite the degeneration of his natural environs, is akin to the "wealth" that Wordsworth later feels from having seen the abundant daffodils. As he puts it in *The Prelude,* "feeling comes in aid of feeling, / If but once we have been strong" (ll. 269–71).

5. For compelling treatment of this relation between Frost and Wordsworth, see Reuben A. Brower, *The Poetry of Robert Frost: Constellations of Intention* (New York: Oxford University Press, 1963), especially chapters 3 and 4. Brower offers many useful formulae, economically rendered—e.g., "Frost's awareness of the temptingly mysterious view of the natural world and his reluctant commitment to a sterner, more realistic view" (76)—and with few exceptions corroborative of my stance in this essay. As will be seen in my discussion of "Directive," I think that Brower, like many of Frost's exegetes, resists the pessimism implicit in his own reading of the poems, but this is perhaps a matter of emphasis rather than flat disagreement. Methodologically, our difference is that Brower intends his consideration of Wordsworth (and Emerson and Thoreau) "not to trace detailed influences. . . . [but] to place the quality of Frost's poetry of natural things" (42). My aims are more specific here, are concerned with detailed influences: or, more accurate, are concerned with each poet's attitude toward the exact question of "influence."

6. Is this, as Harold Bloom would have it, the "anxiety of influence"? Perhaps: yet Frost, whom Bloom claims for his company of "strong" poets, seems not to aggrandize himself by degrading his precursors so much as (if at all) by degrading his successors. Bloom, though often so compelling, seems better to assert his theoretics in respect of poets whose "influence" is unobvious or denied (e.g., Stevens) than of those like Frost who acknowledge it, however crankily. The edition of Frost's poetry quoted from here and throughout the essay is *The Poetry of Robert Frost,* ed. E. C. Lathem (New York: Holt, Rinehart and Winston, 1969, 415–16.

7. William Wordsworth, *Selected Poems and Prefaces,* ed. Jack Stillinger (Boston: Riverside, 1965). All future quotations from Wordsworth's poetry and prefaces are from this edition.

8. Cf. Frost's "The having anything to sell is what / Is the disgrace in man or state or nation" ("New Hampshire") and Wordworth's "Getting and spending, we lay waste our powers."

9. Letter to Charles James Fox (14 Jan. 1801), cited in Wordsworth, *Selected Poems and Prefaces*, 525.

10. My reading of "Michael" is extended in my essay "The Pastor Passes: Wordsworth and His 'Michael,'" *ELH* 45 (1978).

11. David A. Sanders, "Revelation as Child's Play in Frost's 'Directive,'" in *Frost: Centennial Essays*, ed. Jac Tharpe (Jackson: University Press of Mississippi, 1976), 267–74 *passim*. Cf. Reuben Brower, who articulates my view felicitously and accurately—"Being saved is becoming a child again in a scriptural and Wordsworthian sense, but without putting aside later knowledge" (*Poetry of Robert Frost*, 239)—yet immediately reverts to the "idealist" position of Sanders: "it is the *poem* that saves the poet and his readers" (240). By stressing the degree to which "Directive" is "rigamarole," I present what I think is Frost's skepticism toward his own salvational terminology.

12. Letter to Fox, in Wordsworth, *Selected Poems and Prefaces*, 522.

13. *Biographia Literaria* XIV. S. T. Coleridge, *Selected Poetry and Prose*, ed. Elisabeth Schneider (New York: Holt, Rinehart and Winston, 1971), 284–85.

14. For a brilliant comparative study of Frost and Wordsworth, concentrating on the latter's liminal moment of blurred vision as opposed to Frost's manipulation of clear sight, see David L. Miller, "Dominion of the Eye in Frost," in Tharpe, *Frost*, ll. 141–58.

15. Thomas Weiskel, *The Romantic Sublime: Studies in the Structure and Psychology of Transcendence* (Baltimore: Johns Hopkins University Press, 1976), 50.

16. *Selected Prose of Robert Frost*, ed. Hyde Cox and E. C. Lathem (New York: Holt, Rinehart and Winston, 1949), 112. Subsequent references will be cited parenthetically as *Prose*.

17. According to the respective poetic concordances, *sublime* appears in some form in Wordsworth sixty-seven times to Frost's one (ironic) use, in "Kitty Hawk."

18. Frost, "Tribute to Wordsworth," 92.

19. Frost, "Tribute to Wordsworth," 93.

2 principles from his teachers:
   form, 117 (RF)
   feeling, 122 (WW)

Vicarious reading
     (Keats on Chapman, on Lear)

— what I try to do for students —
   what I've done w/ SL, reading
        through JE's eyes.